Case In Point

Graph Analysis for Consulting and Case Interviews

Marc P. Cosentino
Mukund Jain

MBA Analytica

Published by Burgee Press, Santa Barbara, CA

Also by Marc P. Cosentino

Case in Point: Complete Case Interview Preparation

The Harvard College Guide to Consulting

The Harvard College Guide to Case Interviews

The Harvard College Guide to Investment Banking

Edited by April Michelle Davis

ISBN: 978-0-9863707-0-0

First Printing 2015

Printed in the United States

The mind is wondrous. It starts working the second you're born and doesn't stop until you get a case question.

Contents

1 : Introduction

"I was given forty minutes and a deck of twenty-five slides to analyze. I had to reduce the number of slides to seven, redraw them, and then present the case to the interviewer. What are the conclusions and next steps? There were four bubble charts and two bar charts with bars of various heights and widths. I ripped the pack of slides apart, laid them out on the conference table, and then got to work."
— **Harvard Business School student 2015**

We have seen a major increase in the use of charts during case interviews, particularly at the MBA level. No doubt, this will quickly trickle down to the undergraduate, non-MBA, and industry-hire interviews.

Sometimes the charts will be part of a thirty-deck pack that you are expected to analyze and present (BCG and Bain), while other times will be a stand-alone chart that you are to analyze out loud on the fly (McKinsey).

This book was designed to help you not only understand the role of graphs in consulting (both during an interview and on the job), but also analyze 11 types of charts, quickly, completely, and with great confidence.

In today's digital world, we are either providing information, or offering information through our actions with little to no intrusion. For example, when we go to the grocery store and pay for our groceries with a credit card, we are not just providing confidential financial information to enable the transaction. We are also providing valuable data that includes everything from what we are purchasing to when we are purchasing it to where it is stocked on the shelf to how much we are paying for it. All of this data – and more – is stored, aggregated, and analyzed by various parties to inform their respective strategies. The grocery store may use the data to determine where to shelf certain items. The credit card company may use the data to guide their rewards calendar. The individual brands might use this information to refine their respective positioning, guide their pricing, and adjust their promotional calendars. What appeared to be a simple transaction at the grocery store generated highly valuable data that can affect not only our own lives but also the world around us.

Long before the current age of analytics, forward-thinking companies have been using whatever data is available to them to guide their business strategies. Consulting firms have been somewhat instrumental in driving this mindset. Consultancies, whose recommendations are guided by a desire to mitigate risk, realized long ago that the safest path forward for their clients is one guided by the outcomes of decisions made in the past. In other words, there is perhaps no better indicator of future outcomes than historical results applied to the current state. Because historical data is irrefutable, consultancies – armed with this information – construct recommendations grounded in strong foundations, recommendations that are logical and calculated.

While there is a high value placed on data, the proper interpretation and application of data is equally important, if not more important. After all, what good is data if you cannot understand it or, worse yet, cannot use it to guide how you run your business? Thus, businesses and consulting firms alike place a premium on candidates who can not only represent datasets visually in a clear and effective manner (i.e., through graphs), but also, deduce and decode graphs to reveal the phenomenon that is occurring in real life. Although the skill of graphing data is difficult to test in an interview setting, testing a candidate's ability to interpret a graph is certainly not challenging. This fact brings us to the simple mission behind writing this book: to help candidates interpret graphs accurately for successful case interviews.

In today's world, companies collect reams and reams of data. Graphs help organize the data so we can understand what may actually be happening and construct a strategy in response. In other words, graphs pictorially tell a story that would other-wise have been impossible to convey. When created properly, graphs elegantly show the relationship between different sets of numbers using symbols such as lines, bars, wedges, points, or even bubbles. Conversely, a poorly-created graph can mislead the reader to an incorrect interpretation of the data and ultimately to a flawed strategy.

Our hope in writing this book is to educate and prepare the candidate. As such, we have structured the book to benefit all readers. The book starts with an anatomy of a simple graph followed by a framework that we have found to be effective in interpreting graphs. Next are brief sections on the 11 most common types of graphs. Here, we provide a definition of the graph and share an example that we analyze using the framework. We conclude the book with 8 cases to enable the reader to practice graph interpretation skills in a case setting. Please note that the word "graph" and "chart" are used interchangeably in this book.

We hope you find this book to be valuable in your preparation. For us, writing it has truly been a labor of love.

2 : Anatomy of a Graph

Most well-constructed graphs have 7 critical components that facilitate their interpretation. Let's take a look at these through the lens of an actual graph:

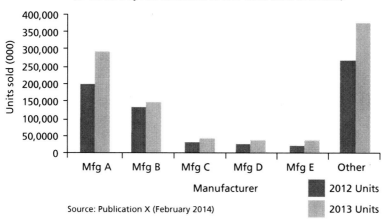

Worldwide Smartphone Sales
(Units Sold by Manufacturer to End Users in 2012 & 2013)

Source: Publication X (February 2014)

1. **Title:** The title of the graph clearly communicates what is being represented by the data at a high level. This graph represents the total number of worldwide smartphone sales.
2. **Subtitle (optional):** The subtitle provides more specificity to the reader regarding what is being presented on the graph. The graph above qualifies the data by showing how many smartphones were sold by each of five manufacturers in two years: 2012 and 2013.
3. **X-axis:** The x-axis usually depicts the factors or variables that are being studied. These factors or elements are also referred to as the independent variables, the phenomena that may have an influence on the dependent variables. In this graph, the factor or variable we want to study is the smartphone manufacturer. We are interested in comparing sales by smartphone manufacturer, labeled Manufacturer.
4. **Y-axis:** The y-axis usually depicts the measurement or value associated with the independent variable. What is represented on the y-axis is sometimes referred to as the dependent variable, the phenomenon that is impacted by the independent variable. Graphs can have 1-2 y-axes, though most have just one. In this example, the y-axis is labeled Units sold (000) and depicts the measurement or value we want to compare across manufacturers. The value for comparison is the number of units sold.

5. **Legend:** The legend provides further clarity on the values depicted on the graph. Because the graph represents sales for two years, each of which is shaded differently, it is important to clarify to the user which set of bars represents which year. This is clearly accomplished by the legend where the light gray bars represent 2013, and the dark gray bars represent 2012

6. **Units:** The units are usually part of each axis' label. They define what is being presented along each axis or the magnitude of the data. In the graph above, the x-axis represents manufacturers and is labeled accordingly. The y-axis represents unit sold in thousands. Thus, each number on the axis is actually in the millions.

7. **Footnote:** Lastly, the footnote provides information pertaining to the source of the data or additional information about the graph. In our example, the data in the graph was published in 2014 in Publication X so if the reader wanted to reference the source, he or she could do so.

Framework

Since you are applying for a consulting opportunity, you know the importance of frameworks. Consulting firms value structured thinking, and frameworks provide the structure needed to organize one's thoughts to solve complex business problems methodically. The business world is replete with frameworks, and here is another one to add to your arsenal – except this one is designed to help you interpret graphs accurately. Constructed based on our own experiences, this 3-step framework is logical so you can easily remember it and draw upon it during your interview.

When presented with a graph, refrain from immediately formulating and articulating a response unless you first run through the following framework. Remember, it is better to be correct than fast and incorrect.

The Ivy Graph Framework: A 3-step approach to interpreting any graph accurately

Step 1: Scan. *Quickly* run through the anatomy of the graph to understand what is being presented.

Graphs in consulting interviews can be overwhelming. After all, they are designed to represent complex datasets. Having an understanding of what the data actually is could not be more important in setting one up for success. Sometimes, the title of the graph and the data presented can help clarify the business challenge.

Step 2: Extract. Distill insights from the graph by first anchoring your interpretation to one data point, one subset of data, or a singular condition and then shifting your focus onto other data points, subsets, or conditions.

Once you understand what is being presented through Step 1, focus your attention on a small segment of the graph – not necessarily visual. Localizing your interpretation allows you to test and refine your insights and hypotheses. Once you feel you have converged on a set of insights, you can move on to the last step.

Step 3: Apply. Apply insights from Step 2 to the business challenge you are trying to solve for your client.

Drawing insights from graphs is just an academic exercise if one cannot apply those insights to the business challenge at hand. So, after you formulate those insights, you have to shift your focus away from the graph and onto the client's overall business. Think of what other information the interviewer has provided until that point. How can you combine that information with the insights you have extracted from the graph to explain what is happening and how the client should move forward? Think about what additional information you need to support your analyses and recommendation.

✛ Line Graphs

The line graph is one of the simplest graphs used in consulting. It is essentially a collection of data points that are connected with a line. As such, a line graph is primarily used to show how a particular value of interest changes over time. What is important to remember is that the data points can be connected to form a line only because time provides *continuity,* and therefore, connecting the data points makes sense. Despite their simplicity, line graphs can be made somewhat complicated with two elements: 1. multiple lines on the same graph and 2. a secondary y-axis.

Having multiple lines on the same graph is an effective way to compare different entities. When multiple lines are on the same graph, they are distinguished by different colors or dashes. Identifying what each line represents is simplified by the legend.

While comparing entities among one variable is important, determining how that variable varies in comparison with another variable of interest may also be critical. A secondary y-axis allows including the second variable on the same graph.

Let's explore the line graph through the following example.

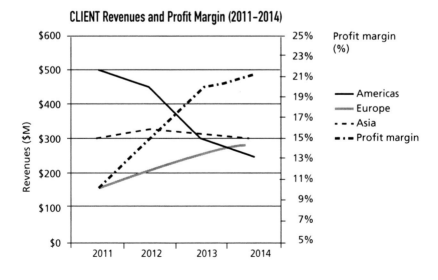

CLIENT Revenues and Profit Margin (2011–2014)

Step 1: Scan. Starting with the title, we can see that the line graph above includes revenues and profit margins – two variables with different units.

The x-axis indicates the progression of time, specifically four years. Because time provides continuity, having lines makes sense. If, for example, the x-axis were different geographic regions, connecting data points across different regions would not make sense as geography does not provide continuity.

Because we wanted to see how revenues and profit margins changed together over time, we needed a secondary y-axis. Without one, it would not be possible to include both of these on the same graph. As we can see from the graph, the y-axis on the left measures revenues while the one on the right measures profit margin.

Next, we see that there are four lines on the graph. Determining what is represented by each line is possible with the help of the legend in the box on the lower right. According to the legend, the first three lines represent revenues for the three geographic regions in which our client operates. Therefore, these lines should be read using the y-axis on the left. The fourth line in the legend represents profit margin. Thus, this line should be read using the y-axis on the right.

Now that we understand the lay of the land, let's dig deeper.

Step 2: Extract. Hypothetically, a line graph depicting only one entity and only one variable is fairly easy to interpret because there is just one y-axis. Even a line graph that includes more than one entity is rather easy to interpret if for all entities we are just measuring one variable because such a graph only has one y-axis. However, if a graph represents more than one variable and thus includes two y-axes, it becomes a challenge to interpret.

To interpret the line graph above, let's start by anchoring our focus on the x-axis – specifically 2011. That year, our client's revenues were disproportionately in the Americas region ($500M out of $1.1B), and our profit margin was about 10%. In 2012, our client's margins rose to 15%. That year saw an increase in revenues in Europe and Asia along with a decline in revenues in the Americas region. The trend continued further in 2013 as revenues out of Europe continued to increase as the Americas region slipped again. Asia was relatively flat. Given Asia's flatness, it appears that margin is more sensitive to what happens in Europe and in the Americas region than what happens in Asia. Finally, in 2014, our client's margin expanded again; however, this time, the increase was smaller. This can be explained primarily by a smaller decline in revenues out of the Americas and a tapering of revenues out of Europe.

While the Americas region contributed nearly 50% of overall revenues in 2011, all three regions had a nearly equivalent contribution in 2014. Furthermore, our client's margin percentage nearly doubled over that time due to the shift in revenue mix.

Based on this data, we can conclude that our client's European business carries a lower cost basis than business in the Americas and so revenue growth in Europe can be achieved without incurring a cost as high as in the Americas. Conversely, reducing operations in the Americas, while lowering overall revenues, shed the business of the high costs in that region – thus achieving overall margin expansion.

Apply: The key insights extracted in the previous section will help guide our client's strategy given its goals and constraints. Given our overall profit margin's sensitivity to business in the Americas and in Europe, these two regions – more than Asia – should be in focus if growing margins is the primary goal. If that is indeed the case, investing in executing strategies in Europe appears to be an obvious path forward if doing so does not alter the cost structure. Simultaneously, our client should explore ways either to reduce its cost structure in the Americas or further curtail operations in this region altogether.

Let's assume that our client wants to grow revenues in 2015 without consideration for profit margin. The obvious move in this case would be to reverse what is being done in the Americas region to reduce revenues. Assuming it is possible to revert to how our client was running the Americas region, we should consider that option to complement the steady growth achieved in Europe.

Conclusion: Because line graphs connect points, the use of a line implies continuity among the points. As such, the x-axis usually indicates the progression of time. Line graphs can show either one or two variables, depending upon what the author wants the reader to focus on during interpretation. Finally, because line graphs can show either one or two variables, they can have either one or two y-axes – one for each variable.

✛ Bar/Cluster/Stacked Bar Graph

A bar graph is a two-dimensional graph that uses vertical or horizontal bars to indicate the value of a particular category. If vertical bars are used, the x-axis includes the various categories, and the y-axis represents the values associated with each category. Bar graphs can also be used to compare components of a whole across multiple categories. Consider the following table of data, which shows a company's revenues across multiple regions.

Region	Revenues ($M)			
	2011	2012	2013	2014
Americas	100	100	150	150
Europe	50	75	50	100
Asia	50	25	50	50

This can be represented through a variety of bar graphs. Total revenues by year can be represented as follows, where the reader has to add up the total for each region. This type of bar graph is known as a cluster bar graph because the various components are clustered along each category, which in this case is the year.

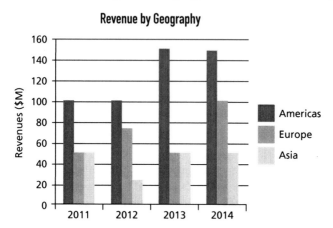

While informative, the cluster bar graph can be challenging to read when it comes to drawing conclusions about the total. That's where the stacked bar graph comes in, named for its appearance. Here, all the components comprising a whole *within* a category are stacked on top of one another. This is a more elegant way to show not only the totals, but also the various components across multiple categories.

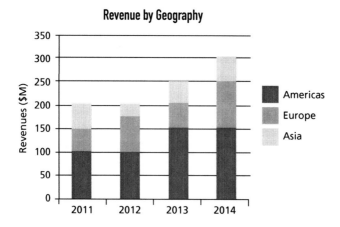

When interpreting a cluster or stacked bar graph, it's important to use the legend to draw insights not only about the totals, but also about the components comprising the totals. Using the stacked bar graph above, let's apply our framework to the analysis.

Step 1: Scan. As the title of the graph indicates, we are looking at our client's revenues across the three regions where it operates. The x-axis displays revenues for four categories or years. The y-axis shows the actual revenues. Each bar shows the revenues broken down by the three regions with the total being the sum of the three regions or the overall "height" of the bar. The legend identifies each region. So, in 2011, our client's total revenues were $200M. The Americas region contributed $100M, Europe contributed $50M, and Asia contributed $50M.

Step 2: Extract. The interpretation of any bar graph occurs at two levels. The first level is *within* a category. In this example, that would be at the individual year level. The second level is <u>across</u> categories or from year to year.

With any type of bar graph, anchoring depends on the configuration of the graph. If the categories are time-based, you should anchor the analysis on the bar representing the earliest time period. If the categories are not time-based, you should start the analysis either on the left-most bar (if the bars are vertical) or the top-most bar (if the bars are horizontal).

In our case, the categories are years and the earliest time period is represented by the left-most bar, which depicts revenues for 2011. So, let's start there. Here we can see that 50% of revenues come from the Americas region, and the other two regions contribute 25% each. As we move to 2012, we can see that the revenue total has remained constant but the revenue split by geography has changed. That is, revenues from Europe have increased from $50M in 2011 to $75M while revenues from Asia have decreased from $50M to $25M. In terms of percentage, revenues in the Americas region continue to make up 50% of total revenues. However, Europe's contribution has increased to 37.5% ($75M/$200M), and Asia's contribution has decreased to 12.5%. Similar analysis can be done for 2013 and 2014.

In general, we can see that overall revenues have increased from 2011 (at $200M) to 2014 (at $300M). Revenues achieved in the Americas region have increased from $100M in 2011 to $150M in 2014, but these revenues still make up 50% of total revenues. Revenues from Europe have also increased over these four years from $50M (25% of total 2011 revenues) to $100M (33% of total 2014 revenues).

Step 3: Apply. These insights should serve us well in addressing our client's business challenge(s). Let's assume that our client wants to grow company revenues through expanding its footprint and is looking for a recommendation on which geography it should select for its expansion. Based on the insights gleaned from this graph alone, one recommendation could be to expand in Europe based on its growth rate ($50M to $100M from 2011 to 2014). We have to balance this recommendation with additional analyses that look at capacity, capabilities, competitive intensity, and profitability. In terms of capacity, we would need to assess whether Europe could actually support growth. We would also have to determine whether we have the capabilities to invest in expansion in Europe. Finally, the graph above does not include profitability numbers. It's possible that profits out of Europe are lower than profits in Asia or the Americas.

Conclusion: The bar graph is a simple way to depict data in a way that makes comparing data easier. When studying a bar graph, it's important to be systematic in one's approach. Start from the earliest bar and look at trends across different categories. The candidate should also be mindful of the legend. Lastly, when observing components comprising the whole, it's wise to convert components into percentages.

✛ Pie Graphs

Like the line graph, the pie graph is one of the simplest graphs used in consulting because it is intuitive to understand. After all, most people have been exposed to a circle that has been divided into wedges, whether through food or in geometry class. Unfortunately, a pie chart's simplicity is also its limitation. A pie chart is used to show the various components of a whole and the relative magnitude of each component. While this information is valuable, it's more easily processed by most people via a bar graph where each component contribution is represented by bars that run parallel to one another and are thus visually easier to interpret. In a pie graph, it's the angle from the center that determines the magnitude, which is harder for the human eye to process. Most pie graphs are one level, but consulting firms sometimes like to test a candidate's ability to interpret multi-level pie charts, which are a set of concentric rings where the size of each item represents its contribution to the inner parent segment.

Let's explore more through interpreting a multi-level pie graph. We'll start with a basic pie graph and work our way up toward the multi-level. Assume our client is a retailer that invests in multi-channel marketing across three platforms: television, print, and online. Their investment in these channels could be represented through the one-level pie chart below.

CLIENT 2014 Marketing Investment by Channel

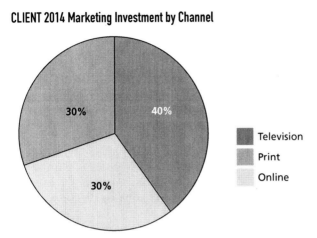

Although the information above is valuable, it is limited. Suppose the client wanted to dig deeper to understand what percentage of the television budget was local versus national. The traditional, one-level pie graph would be limited in conveying this information. That's where the multi-level pie graph below could be helpful.

CLIENT 2014 Marketing Investment by Channel

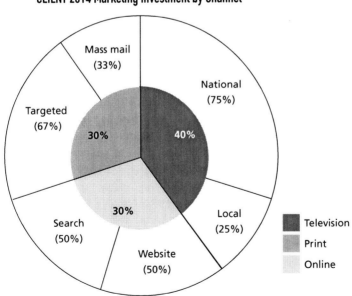

In the graph above, a concentric circle encompasses the original pie graph. This circle outer disaggregates the three major components into their respective components.

ne case of television, there are two components: national and local. ond to the client's television investment.

...ed on the title, the graph shows our client's marketing budget allo- ...on for 2014.

Starting with the inner circle, we see that there are three components – represented in the legend. Each component's size represents the client's allocation towards that marketing channel. If the client's budget was $1M, then television's share would be $400K.

Let's move to the outer ring. We can immediately see that these pieces spatially align with the inner ring. In other words, national and local line up with television, search and website line up with online, and mass mail and targeted line up with print. the percentages in the outer ring represent that segment's contribution to its parent's contribution. in other words, national comprises 75% of the television budget and local makes up the remaining 25%.

One of the benefits of the pie graph – and particularly of the multi-level pie graph – is that it allows the reader to see visually each component's relative contribution to the whole. In scanning the graph, we can see that national television and targeted print represent the two largest marketing allocations for our client.

Step 2: Extract. To interpret a pie chart, it's best to anchor your focus on the largest wedge of the inner-most ring first. As we can see from our example, our client spends more of its marketing budget on television (40%) than on any other channel, though the difference between tv and the other two is not very significant (40% vs. 30% for print vs. 30% for online). What we do not know by looking at this graph is the actual spend. All we know is the relative proportion of that spend (i.e., 4:3:3).

Because this is a multi-level graph, we can now turn our attention to the outer ring. Let's start with television since it's the largest. according to the graph, the investment in television is divided into two: national and local. Again, while we know the relative proportion of these two, we do not know the actual amounts. In this case, 75% of the television budget is allocated for national, and 25% is allocated for local. The size of the segments or wedges reflect that ratio as national is three times larger than local. The other channels can be interpreted similarly. For example, of the 30% print investment, 67% is allocated towards targeted and 33% toward mass mail.

It's worth reiterating that the percentages provided for segments on an outer ring should use the outer segment's next most inner ring as the base. Thus, the actual percentage for television – local is not 25% but rather 25% *of* 40%, or 10%.

Step 3: Apply. Let's assume that our client wants to optimize its marketing investment based on downstream conversion. For example, if research showed that search provides the highest ROI, our recommendation could be to adjust its allocation to invest more in search by reducing its spend in underperforming channels. Similarly, if we wanted a more balanced approach to our marketing, we could adjust the investment accordingly. This particular graph also exposes the pie graph's limitation. If a candidate were presented with this specific graph in an interview, the candidate should ask how investment has shifted over time, what the ROI is in each channel, and how the ROI has changed over time.

Conclusion: The pie chart's value is in its ability to show the various components of a whole in a simple, visually intuitive way. The key to interpreting these graphs is to begin with the largest segment in the inner-most ring first. Once finished with the inner ring, the reader can proceed to the next outer ring. Moving outwards from the center provides structure of thought that will ultimately help the reader better understand the phenomenon being observed.

✛ Area Graphs

The area graph is used to represent how components change over time. This form of representation allows the reader to *make comparisons* among the components as they evolve over time to see how each component's contribution to the whole changes. It is very similar to a line graph except in two ways. First, the area below the line is filled with color to represent volume. Second, unlike a line graph, which just shows each component's individual values, the area graph also shows the sum of all the lines.

To better understand an area graph, let's look at a simple example and apply the Ivy Graph Interpretation Framework. For simplicity, there are only two components in this example, but your case may have more.

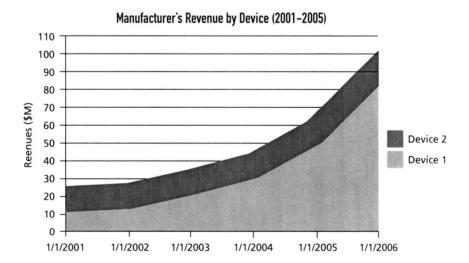

Manufacturer's Revenue by Device (2001–2005)

Step 1: Scan. Based on the title, we're looking at not only a manufacturer's total revenues broken out by the devices that comprise that total, but also how each device's revenue contribution changes over time. Because there are two distinct areas – each represented by a different color – we can conclude that there are two devices. In fact, the legend confirms this. Reviewing the x-axis, we can see that we are looking at a 5-year period (do not let the six marks on the x-axis deceive you). The y-axis represents the manufacturer's revenues in millions of dollars. At a high level, we can see that overall revenues have increased from $25M on 1/1/2001 to $100M on 1/1/2006. What's critical is an understanding of what is driving the significant revenue increase. For that, let's move on to Step 2 of our framework.

Step 2: Extract. Anchoring our interpretation to 1/1/2001, we can see that total revenues were about $25M. It's important to remember that in area graphs, the total can be found by looking at the top of the upper-most band. Each component's contribution is calculated by looking at the difference between the top and bottom of that component's band. For example, Device 1's contribution was $10M since the light gray band starts at $0 and goes up to $10M. Device 2's contribution was $15M as it starts at $10M and ends at $25M – a difference of $15M.

As we extend our analysis from 1/1/2001, we can see that the area representing Device 1 has obviously increased from 2001 to 2006. Because the area represents revenues, we can easily conclude that Device 1's revenues have increased. What can we conclude about Device 2? Have its revenues increased, stayed the same, or decreased from 2001 to 2006? This is a little less obvious because of how our minds work. Most of us – when presented with such a graph – incorrectly look at the thickness of the band in relation to the other band (see the arrow labeled "1" in the chart below) instead of the thickness of the band vertically (see "2" below). Note the obvious difference in the length of the two arrows. If we reorient our eyes vertically, we can see that the Device 2's revenues are also growing. In fact, on 1/1/2005 Device 2's revenues were about $20M, an increase from the $15M we calculated for 1/1/2001. We calculate the $20M by subtracting the bottom of the dark gray band ($45M) from the top of the dark gray band ($65M).

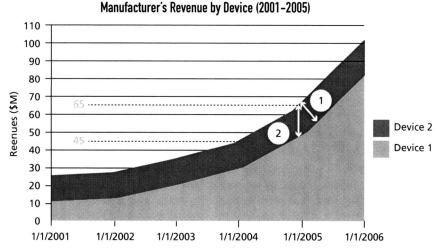

Manufacturer's Revenue by Device (2001–2005)

Since revenues associated with both devices are increasing, we can safely conclude that both are contributing to the manufacturer's overall revenue increase, but because Device 1's area is increasing more rapidly and to a much greater extent than Device 2's, Device 1 is a much bigger contributor to overall revenues than Device 2 – in terms of revenues.

Apply: The application of this insight requires knowledge of our client's business problem. Let's assume that our client wants to make an investment or "big bet" behind just one of these two devices – whether it's to upgrade manufacturing equipment to lower costs or increase sales personnel to drive revenues. On the basis of this area graph alone, we cannot make a recommendation as to which device they should invest in for a number of reasons. First, we need clarity on our client's goals. If the goal is to grow profits, this graph is insufficient as it represents revenue, not profit. While Device 1 is growing more rapidly and to a much greater extent than Device 2 in terms of revenues, Device 1's cost basis may also be significantly higher and costs may also be increasing proportionately to revenues. That is, the manufacturer may already be investing heavily in Device 1 to achieve the revenue growth it is getting, and Device 2's revenues may come from minimum current investment. Second, we have no knowledge of market conditions. Device 1 may be in a more competitive or mature market whereas Device 2 may have slower adoption but could offer significant upside. With these unknowns, any recommendation should be accompanied with caution.

Conclusion: This example illustrates how area graphs enable us to examine how a total and its components change over time. The value of an area graph lies in its ability to enable comparisons among equivalent entities that could either validate previously-made decisions or inform future strategic business decisions.

✦ Scatterplot

A scatterplot is a two-dimensional graph that shows the relationship between two variables. It consists of an x-axis and a y-axis. When graphed, the scatterplot contains a number of dots to indicate each datapoint. The variable plotted on the x-axis is called an explanatory variable, and the variable on the y-axis is called a response variable. Scatterplots are usually used to determine if changes in one variable (i.e., the response variable) can be explained by changes in another variable, namely the explanatory variable. The relationship between the explanatory and response variables can be defined using the following three factors:

1. **Strength.** This describes how strongly the two variables are related. Strength can quickly be determined by looking at how clustered the datapoints are.
2. **Form.** This describes whether there is a relationship between the two variables, and if there is, what shape that relationship takes (e.g., linear, curved, etc.).
3. **Direction.** The direction describes whether the relationship between the two variables is positive or negative.

When interpreting a scatterplot, it's important to characterize the relationship appropriately. If the scatterplot shows a relationship, or correlation, between the two variables, that is all that can be concluded. In other words, correlation does not imply causality. One cannot draw a cause and effect relationship between the two variables.

To help define the relationship along the three factors above, you should try to "smoothen" the datapoints by fitting a line or curve to the data. Possible ways to do this include using a straight line or a parabola.

To better understand a scatterplot, let's look at a practical example. Our client is an energy company with gas stations throughout the United States. In addition to selling gasoline, they sell essential grocery items such as milk, bread, etc.

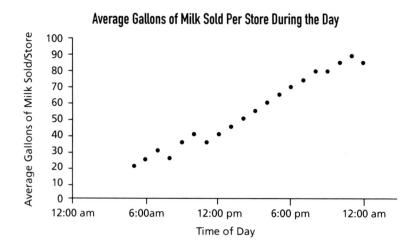

Average Gallons of Milk Sold Per Store During the Day

Step 1: Scan. Based on the title, the scatter plot shows the average gallons of milk sold per store by the hour. The x-axis indicates the time of the day, and the y-axis shows how many gallons of milk were sold on average per store. Therefore, each datapoint on the graph corresponds to the number of gallons sold at that time. We can see that the least number of gallons sold during the day is approximately 20 (at 5 AM) and the most is 90 (at 11 PM). Generally speaking, the number of gallons increases as the day progresses.

Step 2: Extract. Drawing insights from a scatterplot are easier than drawing insights from most other types of graphs. That is because the key insight from a scatterplot is the nature of the relationship between the explanatory variable (along the x-axis) and the response variable (along the y-axis). Thus, you should focus your thinking on the three factors that are used to define the relationship. To answer questions pertaining to those three factors, you should try to "smoothen" the datapoints with a "best fit" line or curve that minimizes distance between the line or curve and the actual point. The graph below shows the best fit line overlayed on the datapoint.

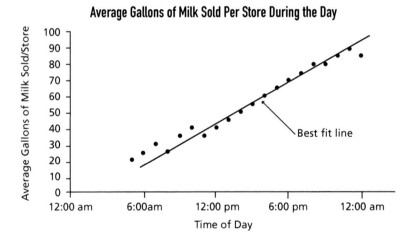

Let's start with strength. The datapoints are fairly clustered and not dispersed so the relationship appears to be strong. Moving on to form, the best fit is linear in nature (vs. a curve), which means the two variables move together. Finally, in terms of direction, the relationship between the two variables is certainly positive moving from left to right. That is, as the number along the x-axis increases (i.e., as it gets later in the day), the values along the y-axis increase as well.

Given these factors, the key insight is that there is a strong positive association between the hour of the day and the gallons of milk purchased.

Step 3: Apply. Now that we know there is a strong positive relationship, we can apply it to solving our client's business challenge. Assume that the client wants to increase grocery-based revenues per store. Knowing that demand for groceries increases later in the day can help us determine what groceries to stock, the shelf space we need, and the quantity to purchase/stock. This information also has significant supply-chain implications, which a strong candidate will bring up to the interviewer.

Conclusion: The scatterplot helps describe the relationship between two variables so we can determine whether changes in the explanatory variable are associated with changes in the response variable. Interpreting scatterplots effectively requires describing the association using three factors: the strength of the association, the form (or shape) of that association, and the direction of the association. Displaying your knowledge of these three factors will position you differently in the eyes of the interviewer.

✛ Bubble Graph

The bubble graph is one that is commonly tested in consulting firm interviews for two practical reasons. First, it is a graph that consultants often use because of its power to represent multiple sets of data elegantly. Second, because interpreting a bubble graph is not inherently easy, interviewers use it to create separation among applicants. As such, learning how to interpret a bubble graph may help you not only land a consulting job, but also succeed at it.

Unlike most graphs, a bubble graph communicates three or more dimensions or variables of data and allows the reader *to make comparisons* visually. Think of a bubble graph as a scatterplot where the size of each point on the graph is proportionate to a third variable or dimension – usually a quantity.

Let's take a look at a simple bubble chart and apply the Ivy Graph Interpretation Framework. For simplicity, there are no numbers in this graph, but expect to see and interpret numbers when you interview.

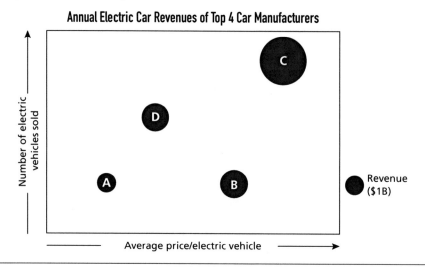

Annual Electric Car Revenues of Top 4 Car Manufacturers

Step 1: Scan. At first glance, based on the title, we're comparing revenues of the top four car manufacturers, but only revenues from sales of their electric vehicles. Because revenues = quantity x price, it makes sense to have these two variables as the x- and y-axis in our graph. Revenues are represented by the magnitude of the bubble. In terms of relative size, C appears to be twice as large as B and D, which appear to be twice as large as A. Let's move on.

Step 2: Extract. Anchoring our interpretation to one manufacturer is a good way to start drawing insights. Because the bubble representing manufacturer C is the largest, let's start there. Because C has the most electric vehicle revenues, we expect it to have either the highest average price/vehicle or the most number of vehicles sold. We can see from the location of its bubble that it has the highest of both. There must be some value in C – whether branding, performance, quality, or other – that allows it to sell more cars at a higher price than other manufacturers.

Moving on, we can see that the bubbles representing B and D are similar, if not identical, in size, indicating that these two manufacturers are equivalent in terms of electric vehicle revenues. What's obviously different about these bubbles is their spatial relationship to one another. B is further to the right on the graph, indicating that the average price of its electric vehicles is greater than D's. Conversely, D is higher on the graph than B, indicating the D has sold more cars. So, while both manufacturers are getting the same revenues, they are doing it in different ways. B charges more per car but sells fewer cars; D sells more cars but at a relatively lower average price. In the absence of additional information, what we cannot conclude is why B can charge more per vehicle or if D is selling more cars because it charges less per car.

Turning our attention to A, we can clearly see that its electric vehicle revenues are the lowest, which is logical given that it sells the fewest cars and charges the least per car.

Apply: When applying these insights, it's important to focus on the business problem facing our client. Let's assume that our client is manufacturer B, and their challenge is to grow revenues. We know that there are two ways to drive revenues: 1. increase price or 2. increase quantity. In the absence of additional information about branding, manufacturing costs, consumer preferences, etc., let's explore both options. Increasing the price is a viable option because the market will bear a higher priced car as evident by manufacturer C's average car price. However, without knowing how C's electric cars differ from B's in terms of branding, performance, quality, and other factors that allow it to command a higher price, we cannot conclude whether we should increase price. All we can say is that the market will bear a higher priced car. However if B wants to grow revenues without consideration of profit, it can either reduce its price (and compromise profit to sell more cars) or build another car similar to D and price it at par with D or higher.

Conclusion: This example illustrates how bubble graphs enable us to make comparisons among different entities across multiple factors or variables. Most other types of charts would not allow such comparisons to be made. For example, if we were to construct a bar graph, with each bar representing a manufacturer, the height of the bar could represent revenues, but we would lose the factors contributing to those revenues, namely average price and number of cars sold.

✛ Radar Graphs

Unlike most graphs, a radar graph displays more than two variables of data elegantly in a 2-dimensional graph. This graph is also known as a spider chart because it contains multiple axes (one for each dimension) that originate from the same point and data plots are connected with straight lines, resembling a spider's web. Radar graphs present the reader with a more comprehensive view into the entity being graphed than other types of graphs, but their true value lies in enabling comparisons to be made among multiple entities along multiple dimensions. As a result, the reader can identify how different entities are similar and dissimilar and understand the magnitude of their similarities and dissimilarities.

Below is an example of a radar graph. In this scenario, our client is a U.S. car manufacturer. Let's take a closer look.

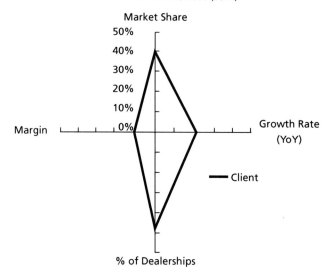

CLIENT's State of the Business (2014)

Step 1: Scan. Based on the title, the graph provides an overview into our client's business in 2014. We can immediately see that there are four primary dimensions which summarize the client's state of affairs: market share, growth rate, % of dealerships, and margin. Here, we can see the power of a radar graph as it provides a lens on multiple variables defining our client at once, something that no other graph can provide. Note that each axis has the same unit of measurement, namely percentage, and that only the markings along one axis (i.e., market share) are labeled, indicating that markings that are equidistant from the origin have the same value. Our legend indicates that only one entity is being represented in this graph, thereby limiting the power of the graph. As the graph stands currently, it is informative, but it paints an incomplete picture making conclusions difficult. What's missing are comparisons with other entities (i.e., competitors). Now consider the revised radar graph, which contains our client's competitors.

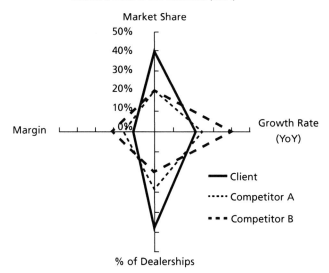

Based on the legend, we can see that this graph includes our client and two competitors, A and B. With all three entities on the same graph, the reader can see the degree of overlap among the three as they all share the same axes.

Step 2: Extract. When it comes to interpreting radar graphs, the reader should anchor on one axis before moving onto the other ones. Let's start with market share. Here, our client has 30% market share whereas each of our competitors have 20%. In terms of growth rate, however, our client lags both competitors. In fact, Competitor B is growing two times faster than our client (40% vs. 20%). Moving clockwise to percentage of dealerships, it's apparent that our client has 50% of all dealerships, clearly exceeding our competitors' respective dealership shares. Lastly, our margins are the lowest among all three at 10%.

Stepping back, we can see that the area of overlap among the three entities is not significant, which means there are clear leaders and laggards in some of the dimensions. For example, Competitor B is the clear winner in terms of growth rate at 40%. Similarly, our client has the highest percentage of dealerships, and its market share is also the highest by a significant amount. In terms of margin, all three entities are bunched together graphically, which implies that the range between the highest and lowest is small (10% for our client and 20% for Competitor B, with Competitor A in the middle at 15%).

Apply: The third and final step of graph interpretation is the application of insights to the client's business problem. Let's assume that our client was evaluating its business in the context of the competitive environment to guide a multi-year strategic plan.

Based on the data above, while our client enjoys a strong market share, its growth rate is the lowest. With Competitor B growing at twice the rate as our client, Competitor B poses a significant threat to our client's market share. Furthermore, having half of all dealerships but growing at only 20% is a cause for concern. Given the relatively flat growth rate, we could conclude that our dealership mix may need to be adjusted to raise our growth. We can do that in various ways such as by closing underperformers or improving them. There are, of course, others, and they need to be evaluated based on overall company goals.

We can also see that our margins trail our competitors' margins. This phenomenon can be interpreted in various ways from exploring our cost structure to assessing our pricing and product mix in our strategic plan. What's particularly noteworthy is the performance of Competitor B, who is not only growing faster than anyone else, but also doing so with fewer dealerships and industry-leading margins. Given their threat, our client may want to explore acquiring Competitor B.

Broadly speaking, our client's business is at risk of losing share. Therefore, any strategic plan must consist of recommendations on preserving and growing share amid fierce competition from players with either a superior cost structure or products that command a price premium that allows them to achieve higher margins.

Conclusion: The radar graph is instrumental in presenting multiple dimensions of data in one graph to enable comparisons to be made among different entities. Interpreting these graphs requires moving systematically from one axis to the next and then stepping back draw broader conclusions.

✛ Boxplot

A boxplot if also called a box and whisker because it consists of a rectangular box with lines extending outwardly from two opposite ends like whiskers on a cat. The boxplot is a way to graph the spread of numerical data – similar to a histogram. Where a histogram provides information about the spread of values in just one group, a boxplot is particularly useful in comparing distributions among several groups or datasets. There are many types of boxplots, but the most common ones found in case interviews depict data through quartiles.

Quartiles are three values that divide the dataset (when ordered from lowest to highest) into four equal groups. The first quartile is the middle number between the smallest number and the median (or middle) number of the entire set. The second quartile is the median. The third quartile is the middle number between the median and the highest value in the dataset. Consider the following set of ordered values: $10M, $15M, $20M, $30M, $80M, $90M, $95M, $100M, and $120M. Let's start with the second quartile since that's the middle number in the entire dataset. Here, our second quartile is $80M. The first quartile (i.e., the middle number between the smallest and the median) is $20M, and the third quartile (i.e., the middle number between the median and the highest number) is $95M.

These values would be graphed in a boxplot as follows:

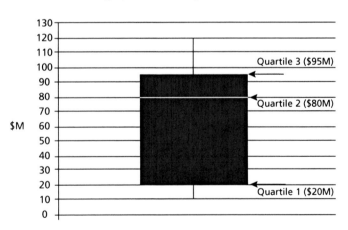

The edges of the box represent the first and third quartile, and the second quartile is represented by a horizontal line inside the box. The lowest ($10M) and highest ($120M) values are represented by the lines that extend out of the box. It's important to remember that unless otherwise stated, the boxplot does not reveal anything about mean (average) or the count.

While the example above depicts the distribution of only one group or dataset, a box-plot usually includes multiple datasets to allow for comparisons. Let's take a look at one for our client, a clothing retailer with stores in North America, Europe, and Asia.

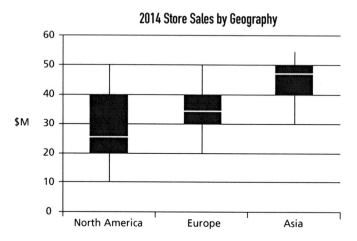

2014 Store Sales by Geography

Step 1: Scan. According to the title, the boxplot shows 2014 sales for our client's stores across three of its geographies. As such, we see three distinct boxplots – one for each geography as indicated on the x-axis. Because this is a boxplot, we immediately know that the data presented reveals the spread of sales across all stores within a particular geography. The amount of sales is depicted on the y-axis in millions of dollars. In North America, for example, the range of sales across all of our client's stores is $10M – $50M.

We also know the values of the first, second, and third quartiles of each boxplot as well as the lowest and the highest values in the range. Because there are three box-plots, we can easily compare store sales across all three geographies.

Step 2: Extract. Unlike most other types of graphs, with a boxplot there is no ideal location at which you should anchor your focus. So, it's probably best to be systematic and start at the left-most end. Analysis of a boxplot occurs at two levels. The first level involves looking at the boxlplot for one geography only. The second level involves comparing geographies.

Starting with North America, we know the range is from $10M – $50M and that the median is at approximately $25M. The first quartile is at $20M, and the third is at $40M. In the case of Europe, sales range from $20M – $50M. The first quartile is at $30M, the second at $35M, and the third at $40M. Store sales in Asia range from $30M – $55M; the first quartile is at $40M, the second is at $48M, and the third is at $50M.

Looking across geographies, we can see that 50 percent of stores, as represented by the box, is spread widest in North America. In Europe and in Asia, 50 percent of all stores (represented by the box) fall within a $10M band. Thus, Europe and Asia have higher density. In other words, store sales are bunched up in Europe and in Asia whereas store sales are more spread out in North America.

In addition to the spread, we can learn a great deal from the sales associated with the respective bands. That is, in North America, 50 percent of stores have sales from $20M – $40M. In Europe, this number is $30M – $40M, and in Asia, this number is from $40M – $50M. Thus, we can conclude that our client's stores in Asia are outperforming their counterparts in Europe and North America. Similarly, our client's stores in Europe are – for the most part – outperforming its stores in North America.

Step 3: Apply. Armed with these insights, we should be able to apply these to solving our client's business challenge(s). Let's assume that our client wants to grow company revenues. One recommendation could be to assess whether or not the Asian or European markets could support more stores since stores in these locations have strong revenues. Another recommendation would be to understand the inconsistent performance across stores in North America. It's important to remember that the graph does not include averages for each geography or the number of stores in each region. This information would also be very valuable in developing a perspective.

Alternatively, if our client wishes to drive profitability, we should ask the interviewer to provide us with cost and profitability information that we could overlay onto this chart to help us determine if closing stores might be a worthwhile undertaking. Without this additional data, we will not be able to arrive at a substantiated recommendation. Perhaps stores in North America are more profitable because of a lower cost basis. Perhaps competitive intensity in Asia will drive down future top line growth.

Conclusion: The boxplot is valuable in depicting the spread or distribution of data not only in one dataset but also across multiple datasets, thus allowing comparisons to be made. While the boxplot provides tremendous insights, it's important to understand that boxplots have their limitations. Interpreting boxplots requires focusing on the range and density of an individual dataset and then the range, density, and values of the range across multiple datasets.

✛ Waterfall Graphs

A waterfall graph represents how a *single measurable cumulative value* is affected as positive or negative inputs are introduced *sequentially*. In so doing, the waterfall visually and numerically allows the reader to examine the sequential effect of intermediate values on the cumulative value. While similar to other graphs in depicting the contribution of components on the whole, the waterfall graph shows both the positive *and* negative effect of the *intermediate* values, a phenomenon lost in other graphs.

To underscore the benefit and the power of a waterfall graph, let's take a closer look through the following illustrative example.

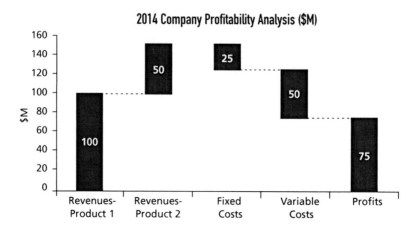

Step 1: Scan. A quick read of the title indicates that we are presented with a graphical analysis of a company's profitability. Thus, we expect to see revenues and costs in the graph. Looking at the x-axis, we can see the key components comprising the company's profits: revenues, fixed costs, and variable costs. The y-axis indicates the value of each of these components in millions of dollars, as indicated by the units in parentheses. There are five bars on the graphs, each associated with a variable in the profit equation: Profits = Revenue $_{Product\ 1-n}$ – Cost $_{fixed\ and\ variable}$. A closer examination of the x-axis shows that the company has two products driving revenues, represented by the first two bars. Total costs are also broken out in terms of fixed and variable (i.e., the third and fourth bars, respectively). The fifth bar represents our singular measurable cumulative value, namely profits.

Step 2: Extract. Unlike most other graphs, waterfalls should be read unidirectionally because the sequence of the various bars is relevant to the story. This makes anchoring our interpretation to either the left-most or the right-most bar an obvious starting point. Returning to our example, if we read it from left to right, we can see that the various components of the graph align with our profit equation. That is, we start out with revenues from two products that in aggregate equal $150M. These bars take our total upwards to $150M. From this total, we subtract fixed costs ($25M) and variable costs ($50M), bringing profits to $75M. Subtractions are represented by bars that reverse the overall direction of the graph.

Reading waterfalls from one end of the graph to the other provides context and allows us to see how the cumulative value is arrived at methodically. If we were to anchor our interpretation near the middle (at the fixed costs), we would lack context and therefore the $25M number would just be a disembodied number.

From this graph, what can we conclude about the overall business? Looking at the size of the bars, we can see that Product 1 is a greater contributor to overall revenues than Product 2. We can also see that our variable costs are twice as high as our fixed costs.

Apply: Without additional insight into the business problem we are trying to solve, let's assume that our client wants to increase profit margin by focusing on costs. Here, given the relative magnitude of the two costs, we should begin by exploring opportunities to reduce our variable costs. Questioning our interviewer about the effect of reducing variable costs on revenues will help guide our overall recommendation. That is, which variable costs appear to be out of line? How will reducing our variable costs affect Product 1 and Product 2 revenues? For example, if a 25 percent reduction in variable costs will reduce our overall revenues by 5 percent, we should explore the practical feasibility of such a move. Once we have traversed this path with variable costs, we should shift our focus to fixed costs. With a similar line of questioning, we can assess the feasibility of changes that would reduce our fixed costs and evaluate the effect of those changes on our profit margin.

Conclusion: The waterfall's value lies in its ability to show how a particular value is affected by different factors sequentially. As such, the key to interpreting waterfalls is having linearity in reading them. Going from left to right or vice versa will help us construct a mental narrative of what we are presented with and understand the phenomenon we are observing. This will, in turn, enable us to focus on responding to the questions we are asked by the interviewer quickly.

✛ Histogram

A histogram is a type of graph that represents the frequency or distribution of a particular observation. In other words, it graphically tells the reader how many times each event occurs. As such, it shows how spread out the data is and whether it is skewed. It consists of an x- and y-axis where the x-axis lists all the possible observations or events, and the y-axis describes the frequency or count of occurrences of each possible observation or event.

Let's look at the following example to get a better understanding of the histogram.

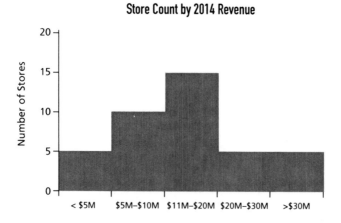

Store Count by 2014 Revenue

Step 1: Scan. The title on the graph above indicates that the graph is displaying the spread of the number of stores by 2014 revenues. Revenues are presented along the x-axis and divided into five bins or ranges. The boundaries of the ranges depend on what the author is trying to prove with the graph. The y-axis indicates the number of stores with revenues in each of the bins. In other words, there were five stores with under $5M of revenues in 2014, ten with revenues between $5M and $10M, and so on. Based on the shape of the graph, it appears that most of the stores had revenues under $20M. In addition to telling us the spread of the data, the graph tells us the total number of stores. We can calculate that easily by adding up the number of stores in each bin. In this case, there are forty stores. If the bins had exact numbers rather than a range, we could calculate an average calculating the total revenues and dividing by 40.

Step 2: Extract. What is most challenging about interpreting a histogram is coming up with a narrative, but if we anchor the analysis on the tallest bar, developing this narrative can be simplified. This approach can also help us draw insights about the data. In our example, the tallest bar is for $11M – $20M with 15 stores. So, our narrative becomes, "There are 15 stores in our footprint with annual revenues between $11M and $20M." What we've also learned through this is that there are more stores with revenues $11M – $20M than any other revenue range. In addition, we can see that there are ten stores with revenues greater than $20M and 15 stores with revenues less than $11M. This gives us an indication about the distribution of our stores in terms of revenues.

It is possible that the interviewer may ask you estimate the average revenue per store. As mentioned in the section above, calculating the average requires estimating the total revenues since we the average would be total revenues divided by the total number of stores, which in this case is 40. Because each of the bins has a range of revenues, we should ask the interviewer if we can estimate the revenues for each of the bins. When presented with a range, it is usually safe to use the midpoint. So, for "< $5M," we can use $2.5M, for "$5M – $10M," we can use $7.5M, and so on. For ">30M," there is no maximum so we should use $30M. Once we have the exact number for each bin or range, calculating the average becomes an easy exercise. The table below summarizes this calculation.

	Estimated revenue for bin	Number of stores	Total revenues
< $5M	$2.5M	5	$12.5M
$5M – $10M	$7.5M	10	$75M
$5M – $10M	$15M	15	$225M
$5M – $10M	$25M	5	$125M
$5M – $10M	$30M	5	$150M
Total		40	$587.5M
Average	$14,687,500		

From this graph, what can we conclude about our client's stores? Based on the height of the bars and the corresponding revenue ranges, it seems that our client has a few stores that are doing quite well and a few that are performing poorly, but the majority are bunched in the middle.

Step 3: Apply. A plausible challenge facing our client could be how to achieve top-line growth. With the goal to grow revenues and only this information available to us, there are several recommendations that we can make. First, we can recommend store-specific strategies that will enable stores in each bin to "move" – in terms of revenues – to a higher-revenue bin. That is, how can we improve stores with revenues < $5M to become stores with revenues ranging from $5M to $10M? Second, we can recommend strategies at the portfolio level by suggesting layering each store's geography onto this analysis to understand what factors are contributing to revenues. If stores with strong revenues are in geographies that can support having additional stores, we might suggest increasing our store count in healthy geographies.

If growing profits were our client's goal, our recommendations could be different depending upon each store's profitability and cost structure. In this case, we should ask the interviewer for this data since that would help guide our recommendations.

Conclusion: A histogram shows the distribution or spread of the data. It allows the reader to see if there are any data points that are outliers, which could illustrate an interesting phenomenon. The key to interpreting a histogram is to start with the tallest bar to test the narrative and then move left or right from there.

✛ Marimekko Graphs

Visually, the Marimekko is one of the most complicated looking graphs in an interviewer's collection. However, after reading this section, you will have a better understanding of how to interpret it, positioning you for a successful interview.

The Marimekko is essentially a collection of stacked bar graphs that have been combined to provide a more comprehensive picture. Like a stacked bar, a Marimekko indicates the contribution of the various contributions comprising a whole. As such, each axis ranges from zero to one-hundred percent.

To understand a Marimekko, it might be better to see how one is constructed. Let's assume that our client manufactures electronics in three categories: kitchen appliances, video, and audio. If we wanted to see how our overall sales are split among these categories by percentage, we would construct the following stacked bar graph below.

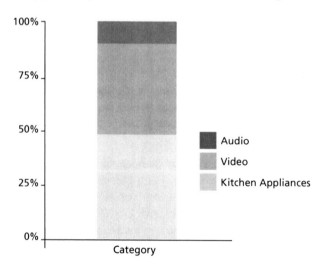

Now suppose we wanted to know how sales *within* each category were split by the products in each of the categories. This is accomplished through the Marimekko graph.

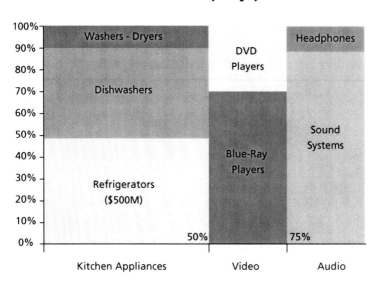

Contribution to 2014 Sales by Category and Product

Step 1: Scan. As the title indicates, the graph shows how the company's overall sales in 2014 is divided by category and product.

Starting with the x-axis, we can see that there are three distinct sections, each of which represents a particular category. The categories are not equally divided because the width of each component along the x-axis of a Marimekko is proportional to its contribution to the horizontal total.

The y-axis is labeled in terms of percentages. If we look at the stack vertically for each category, we can see the products *within* that category, with the height of each product representing its contribution (in terms of percentage) to *that category's* total.

One of the benefits of the Marimekko is that it allows the reader to see visually each component's relative contribution to the whole through the size of each rectangle. In scanning the graph, we can see that refrigerators have the greatest contribution to the company's overall sales.

Finally, note that while each axis is in terms of a percentage, we have enough information to calculate the sales amount because we know the sales contribution of one component, namely refrigerators ($500M).

Step 2: Extract. To interpret a Marimekko systematically, we should begin by anchoring our focus on the x-axis. As we can see from our example, kitchen appliances comprise 50% of our client's sales whereas the other two categories make up 25%

each. What is not explicit are the actual sales numbers for each of these categories, but let's table that calculation for the time being and turn to the y-axis.

Focusing on just the kitchen appliances category, we can see that there are three products in this category as each product is represented by a different colored block whose height corresponds to that product's contribution *within* that category. In the case of kitchen appliances, refrigerators make up 50 percent of sales *within* this category, dishwashers make up 40 percent of sales, and washers-dryers make up 10 percent of category sales. The same interpretation can be made of the products in the other categories.

Because we know sales associated with one of the graph's components, namely refrigerators, we can calculate sales for every product and category in the graph. We know refrigerators make up 50% of kitchen appliances, so kitchen appliances as a category make up $1B of sales. Furthermore, dishwashers make up $400M, and wash-er-dryers make up $100M.

Now that we know kitchen appliances make up $1B of total sales, we can calculate the total sales associated with the other two categories as well. Because kitchen appliances' $1B in sales amounts to 50% of total sales, as indicated on the x-axis, our client's sales across all three categories must be $2B. Thus, total sales for video and audio must be $500M (25% of $2B) each.

Finally, knowing the total for each category allows us to determine the sales for the other products. For example, since Blu-ray players make up 70% of video sales (from the graph), and Video sales are $500M, Blu-ray players contribute $350M of sales (70% of $500M). Furthermore, DVD Players contribute $150M (30% of $500M).

Stepping back, we can see that, as a category, kitchen appliances contribute the most to our company's sales. In terms of products, however, refrigerators have the largest contribution.

Apply: Applying the information requires context, and in the absent of context, we can only guess what the client's business challenges are.

Let's assume that our client wants to grow revenues. Let's further assume that refrig-erators are our fastest growing product segment with sales increasing year-over-year. If we had to make a recommendation on where our client should invest to acceler-ate growth, refrigerators would be an obvious choice. If, however, the refrigerator segment was not growing, or if its growth was exceeded significantly by another segment, we might recommend the faster-growing segment. In such a situation, we might want to ask the interviewer additional questions pertaining to industry trends, our value proposition, our cost structure, etc.

While it is true that refrigerator contribute the most to our client's overall sales, it is unclear how profitable that segment is, both in terms of dollars and margin. If margin expansion is our goal, asking the interviewer questions on segment-level profitability or even asking for a similar graph in terms of profits would inform our recommendation.

As we examine the graph through a broad lens, we can see that the video and audio categories have two products each with one product contributing at least 70% towards its category's total sales (i.e., Blu-ray contribute 70 percent toward video sales, and sound systems contribute 90% toward audio sales). These disproportionate numbers could be a cause for concern for our client. A more balanced product port-folio, if possible, could mitigate risk against a competitor who is taking our share in one of these product segments.

Conclusion: The Marimekko, while appearing complicated, is simply a set of stacked bar graphs creatively combined. Think of it as an elegant way of showing contri-butions of different components of a whole first horizontally and then vertically. By representing the contribution amount of components based on their size, the Marimekko enables comparisons to be made among different entities more easily.

3 : Cases

To punch above your weight in a chart-heavy case interview, you need to practice. By reading through the cases in this section, it will allow you to quickly interpret the information, draw accurate business insights, and apply those insights to solve the client's business problem.

These cases include a variety of graphs and are designed to model actual cases administered in consulting interviews. As you go through the cases, stop and analyze the graphs, and then compare your thoughts to what we determined. We hope you find these helpful in strengthening your preparation.

✛ Case 1: M&A

Our client is a national airline offering routes throughout the United States. They have been around for over 50 years and have grown both organically as well as through mergers and acquisitions. They are looking to drive revenues and have hired us to determine whether they should acquire a competitor airline, and if so, which one.

To summarize, our client is a national airline whose business challenge is to increase revenues. They are exploring acquiring a competitor airline. The client wants to know if they should make an acquisition and, if so, which airline they should acquire. Is that correct?

    – That's right.

Are there any other objectives I should be concerned with?

    – No.

I'd like to take a moment to layout my thoughts.

The student takes a moment to layout his structure.

I'd like to look at three major items. First, I'd like to look at the company and their revenues and profits for the last three years. I'd like to know how much cash they have on hand and whether they are in a position to issue debt. Second, I would like to know about the industry, its growth rate, major players and their market share, and third, the possibility of an acquisition. Is there a competitor who we can afford and who is a good fit, both culturally and strategically?

    – Good. Where do you want to start?

I want to understand how our client's performance is trending. What are their revenues over the past five years?

– Here is a graph showing just that.

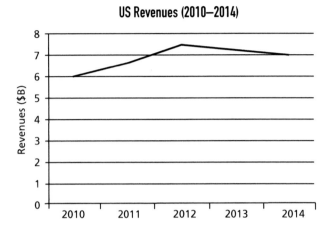

US Revenues (2010–2014)

It appears that we were growing steadily from 2010 to 2012 and then started to trend downward after that. I'd like to dive deeper into this.

– What do you think is happening?

Assuming that the industry has been growing steadily throughout these five years, it seems that the revenue loss is indicative of a loss of market share. That could be because of something internal – for example a decline in quality causing customers to go elsewhere – or external, such as a competitor taking market share. How has our market share changed over this time period?

– Glad you asked. Let me share a graph showing that.

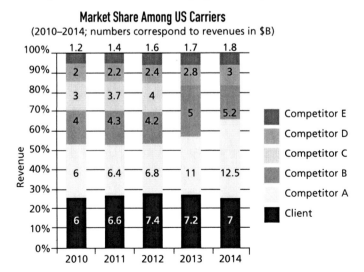

Market Share Among US Carriers
(2010–2014; numbers correspond to revenues in $B)

The student takes thirty seconds to study the graph and make some notes.

Based on this graph, here's what I think may be happening:

1. Overall, the industry is expanding as evident by the increase in overall revenues from $22.2B in 2010 to $29.5B in 2014. Which is about a 25% increase.
2. Every airline's share has steadily increased except our client's. While our revenues have increased, for the most part, our share has declined.
3. In 2010, there were six competitors, but today there are five.
4. It seems as if there was consolidation in 2013 since Competitor C, which was growing up to 2012, doesn't exist.
5. Since Competitor A's market share increased significant in 2013, I would guess Competitor A acquired C.

   – That's right. In 2013, A acquired C, catapulting it into the leadership position in the industry. So what do you think?

I think this industry is one with a lot of consolidation so I'm not surprised our client is thinking about acquiring a competitor. Before going down that path, I'd like to understand if there are segments of our business where we're steady and segments where we're declining.

   – Can you clarify what you mean?

Well, is there a customer segment that we're losing? For example, have we lost ground on the business traveler segment?

   – Internally, the client looked into its customer base, and it appears that revenues from business travelers as a percentage of our overall revenues have remained constant.

Ok. If our mix is constant, are there certain regions of the country where we're losing share?

   – Good question. Take a look at this chart, and let me know what you think.

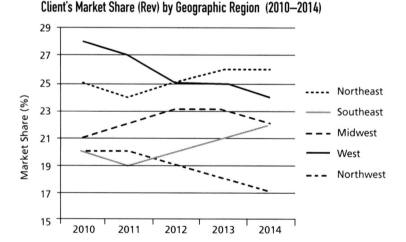

Client's Market Share (Rev) by Geographic Region (2010–2014)

This is very interesting and revealing. Our market share has increased from 2010 to 2014 in the Southeast, the Northeast, and the Midwest, albeit to varying degrees. However, our share has decreased significantly in the West and Northwest, especially in 2012 and afterward. I'm assuming we've lost share to Competitor A who had consolidated with Competitor C. Their merger alone should not have impacted our share, though.

– That's right. What other reasons could there be?

Well, if there are fewer competitors with fewer routes in those regions, it's possible that Competitor A is not facing pricing pressure. Secondly, it's possible that A's customer service is superior to regional players, allowing it to earn a disproportionate amount.

– That's fair. So what do you think our client should do?

Based on the graph above, I'd like to explore competitors for a potential acquisition and would like to know which have a strong presence in the West and Northwest regions of the country. I'd like to know what the route overlap is between our client and our competitors in those regions. Finally, which competitors are profitable?

– Ok, consider the following graph. Does this help you with your recommendation?

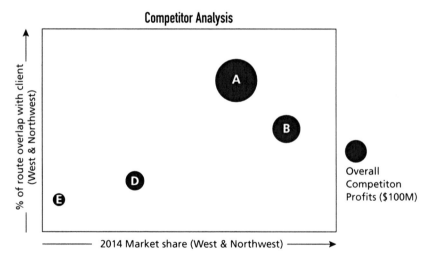

Yes. This is exactly the data I needed. For us to identify the competitor our client should pursue, it's important to weigh the pros and cons of each choice. Competitor A is our primary competitor and the industry leader. As such, we're not going to be able to acquire them. On the other end, Competitor E's advantage is that there is little overlap between its routes in the regions and our routes, which would expand our footprint. However, Competitor E has little market share in the region so acquiring it wouldn't benefit it as much as acquiring B or D. While Competitor D is a good fit because there is not much overlap in its routes and ours, it too has little market share. That brings us to Competitor B. While there is relatively more overlap between B and our client, B's market share is significant. Even if the overlap is 50%, B's high market share more than offsets that overlap. So, my recommend would be to attempt to acquire Competitor B.

> – Any concerns about acquiring B?

Sure. Can we afford it? I have no idea about our financial situation. Also, will the FAA allow a merger if the overlap is that great. Will they impose restrictions on us or force us to sell certain routes to maintain healthy competition?

> – Okay, good. Can you summarize your thoughts for me?

Sure. Given the desire for profitable growth, my recommendation for our client would be to acquire an airline whose acquisition would be complementary to us. Because we are losing share in the West and Northwest regions, I would like to pursue Competitor B whose strengths in these markets would address our weaknesses there. Competitor B is also a good choice because their growth and profitability attest to the health of their business. A risk might be pushback from the FAA.

+ Case 2: Investment Strategy

Our client is a highly profitable pharmaceutical company who has several blockbuster drugs in the diabetes therapeutic category, an area selected because of the founder's personal connections to the condition. They attribute their success to their R&D teams, whose efforts have led to drugs with better efficacy than competitor products. Having achieved this high level of success, they are interested in expanding the business and are looking to us to advise them on where they should focus their R&D efforts in terms of therapeutic category.

To summarize, our client is a pharmaceutical company with a great R&D infrastructure. They have achieved success in diabetes and want to grow organically through R&D efforts in another therapeutic category. They are looking to us to advise them in which category they should focus so they can produce their next blockbuster drug. Is that accurate?

> – That's right.

Can I have a moment to layout my structure?

> – Absolutely.

This is what I'm thinking. I'd like to look at the client first. How big are they in terms of revenue and market share? Do they have any other products besides the diabetes product? Do they have the production facilities and R&D talent to expand into another drug line? Basically, do they have the ability to succeed in that category – not only in terms of their assets and capabilities, but also in terms of the competitive landscape? Next I'd like to look into the pharmaceutical industry, major players, market share and growing therapeutic categories. Third, I know you said they want to grow organically, but we might take a quick look at other ways to enter a growing market. Where would you like me to start?

– What do you want to know about the industry?

I'd like to start by learning more about the major therapeutic categories, how big and competitive they are, how fast they are growing, and how profitable they are. That'll help me figure out the size of the opportunity.

– That sounds like a good plan. Here's a breakdown of the pharma industry.

Theraputic Categories (US revenues–USD)

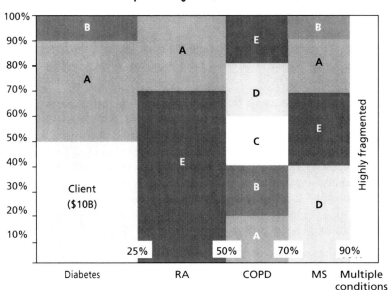

According to this graph, the US pharmaceutical industry is about $80B and 90% of revenues come from four large categories. Because getting a drug into market takes a few years, can you see how these categories have grown and what their growth projections are?

– You're absolutely correct. Taking a drug from formula to testing to the shelf takes about five years. I like where you're going with this. Take a look at this graph.

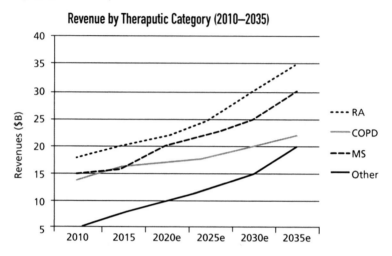

So, it appears from this graph that RA and MS have similar trajectories with RA having a slightly higher upside in terms of total revenues. What's driving the growth for each of these categories?

– Good question. RA stands for rheumatoid arthritis. With an aging US population, RA is projected to be more prevalent. MS is multiple sclerosis. Its growth is driven by better and earlier diagnosis techniques. Previously, it was either undiagnosed or diagnosed too late so the number of cases has historically been undercounted. COPD is chronic obstructive pulmonary disease, which is a group of lung diseases that block airflow and make it difficult for people to breathe. This condition is still growing but slowed in part by fewer people smoking and being exposed to second-hand smoke. The other category has a bunch of conditions and probably isn't worth exploring further.

Ok. This is helpful background. What can you tell me about the profitability of these conditions? That is, what is the customer lifetime value of the drugs currently in these categories?

– The lifetime value of an MS drug is about $50K. For RA, it's about $40K, and for COPD, it's about $25K.

Ok. Based on all the information, I don't think we should pursue COPD as a category. The growth is slowing and the lifetime value is not as high as the other conditions. Moreover, it's a highly competitive category so it might be difficult to crack. Based on growth potential, lifetime value, and competitive intensity, RA and MS seem like better options, relatively speaking. I'd like to dive deeper into each of these conditions. RA has two competitors. How do their drugs differ in terms of efficacy, and how are they perceived by patients and doctors?

– Competitor E's RA drug is superior to A's drug in terms of efficacy, but patients on E's drug have experienced more side effects than patients on A's drug. Most patients who have taken both prefer E because they respond better to it and tolerate unwanted but minor complications. Both drugs are infusions, which means the patient receives it via an injection at the doctor's office. We do know from research that patients would prefer an oral administration of the drug versus the injection.

That feels like an opportunity. If our client's scientists can create a drug that can be taken orally, it'll create a unique and differentiated value proposition for us. I assume the competition is trying to come up with oral solutions as well. What can you tell me about our client's strength in the diabetes category? What about our client's drug has enabled us to achieve a 50% market share?

– Our client's diabetes drug has the best efficacy as well as the least amount of side effects. As a result, more doctors prefer writing prescriptions for it than for any other diabetes drug.

So, is it safe to say our client is better at R&D than the competition?

– In diabetes, our client is superior. I'm not sure that will translate into other categories.

That's fair. What can you tell me about the MS space? There are four manufacturers with competing drugs. How do these drugs differ in terms of efficacy, and how are they perceived by patients and doctors?

– Competitor D has the greatest share because it's been around the longest. Competitor A, D, and E have drugs that require administration via injection. The patient doesn't have to go to the doctor's office, which is convenient, but studies show most patients don't like sticking themselves with a needle. Competitor B's drug is revolutionary in that respect. It is the first ever orally-administered MS drug, which solves a major consumer problem. It has only been in the market for one year. In terms of side effects, all the drugs are fairly equivalent.

Given B's point of differentiation, its share is going to grow significantly in the near future, at least until there is another competitor with a strong oral medication. I'd like to do some math to arrive at my recommendation. I'll start with the RA space.

The student takes a minute to draw up his chart.

RA

	Market ($B)	Share captured (%)	Revs. to Client ($B)
2020e	$22	3.0%	$0.6600
2025e	$25	5.0%	$1.2500
2030e	$30	7.0%	$2.1000
2035e	$35	10.0%	$3.5000

Based on the data, we know what the size of the market is projected to be. That's what I've got in the first second column. In the second column, I'm estimating the share we might be able to capture. Since Competitor E has a superior product, I don't think we can affect their 70% share. The upside for us lies in stealing share from Competitor A, which might be difficult but not insurmountable, which is why I've estimated a slow, conservative penetration trajectory capped at 10%. This assumes we enter the market with an offering that is as good as A's drug but not better than E's drug. I'll do the same with MS.

MS

	Market ($B)	Share captured (%)	Revs. ($B)
2020e	$20	5.0%	$1.000
2025e	$22	7.0%	$1.540
2030e	$25	10.0%	$2.500
2035e	$30	12.0%	$3.600

With MS, I'm estimating that we can capture a greater share of the market because three of the four competitors are at parity, and B's drug is the one that's probably going to achieve the fastest growth since it's the only oral medication. Because B only has 10% of the market, there is more share up for grabs. Thus, I'm projecting more aggressive share capture numbers here.

    – I like the thinking and the rationale, but what else do you have to consider.

There are a couple of other factors. First, do we have the expertise to formulate a drug in the MS space? Secondly, are there any patent implications at play? In other words, are any of our competitors' drugs about to have their patent expire? If that's the case, it could unlock even a bigger opportunity for us.

    – Those are all valid considerations. So what is your recommendation?

Based on the current market conditions and growth projections, my recommendation for our client would be to prioritize the MS category for expansion rather than the RA category. RA appears to be a steady duopoly whereas in MS, we have a better chance to take share. In terms of market entry, I can think of four ways. First, our client can explore buying out Competitor B's drug. Second, our client can evaluate co-promoting B's drug, a practice that is common in the pharma space. Third, buying another competitor's drug could be an option if their drug can be reformulated to be administered orally. Four, our client can R&D its own MS drug. Let's look at each of these options.

Option one could be a significant financial investment that may not ultimately be profitable for our client. Co-promoting B's drug could be viable if our client could add value in the relationship that Competitor B desires. It's also the quickest way to enter the market. Buying another competitor's drug and reformulating it could work if our client has the capabilities to reformulate it. It's possible that redesigning it requires a greater investment than developing it in-house, which is the fourth option. Options three and four, however, would delay market entry.

In summary, I would evaluate each of these four options in terms of ROI and time horizon.

✛ Case 3: Improve Profit Margin

Our client is a large industrial conglomerate. We're working with their water technology division that has reverse osmosis facilities to purify water for commercial use. For the past two years, their profit margins have remained flat. They would like to understand why margins have plateaued and what they can do to improve.

To summarize, our client is the water technology division of a large conglomerate looking to improve their profit margins after two flat years. They want to understand why margins have flattened and how they can improve them. Is that accurate?

– That's right.

The student takes a moment to write out her notes.

– Thanks. I'd like to dive deeper into the both the revenues as well as the costs - both fixed and variable to isolate the causes. I would then like to explore the different options that can achieve the level of margin expansion they want.

– That sounds like a plan.

What were our revenue streams over the last three years?

– Here's a graph that might help.

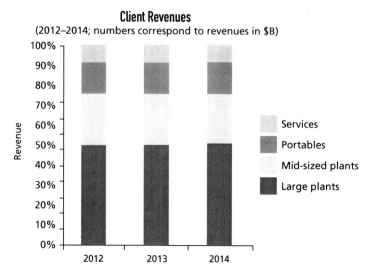

Client Revenues

(2012–2014; numbers correspond to revenues in $B)

Thank you.

She takes a moment to scan the graph and make some notes.

According to the graph, our revenues are growing by about 5% in our largest two revenue sources – large plants and mid-sized plants. Portables and services are flat. Overall, though, our revenues have increased from $24B in 2012 to $25.8B, which is about 3.6% year-over-year or 7% over two years. How does that compare with pre-2012 numbers?

– The revenue numbers are in line with historical performance. Large and mid-sized plants have always accounted for 70 – 75% of total revenues. The other two revenue streams have always hovered around recent numbers.

Can you share our cost breakdown: fixed and variable?

– Sure. Here's the 2014 cost breakdown.

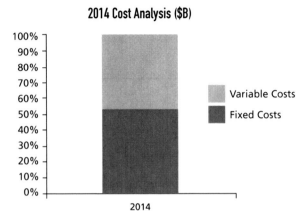

Thank you. Can you provide a breakdown of our fixed and variable costs? I'd like to understand what's having the greatest impact on our profitability.

– Here is a breakdown of our 2014 fixed costs across all our streams (large, mid-sized, portables, and services).

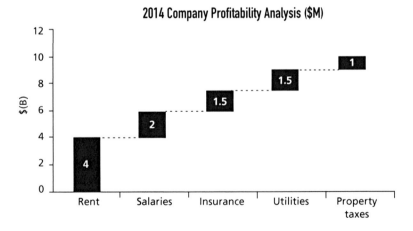

As expected, costs associated with our facilities make up the bulk of our expenses. How have these costs changed over time?

– These costs have actually remained steady the past several years.

I see. How many large sized facilities do we have, and can you tell me how profitable they are? I'd like to explore if there is a way to affect the business positively by closing large-sized facilities that are underutilized or unprofitable. Presumably the large-sized facilities would reduce our fixed costs the most.

– You're right in that large-sized plants carry the bulk of our costs. Here is a map of the country. The circles indicate where our large plants are located. The positive circles indicate plants that are profitable and the negative circles indicate plants that are unprofitable.

According to the graph above, there are four unprofitable large-sized plants. Why are we still keeping these unprofitable facilities? Is there a strategic reason? Is it because of legacy?

– Great question. Historically, the industry was highly fragmented so our client built large-sized plants in some areas to keep out the competition. Over time, there has been quite a bit of consolidation and a number of players have exited because of reduced demand in some areas, leaving our client with large-sized plants in areas that have become unprofitable.

Ok. So what I would recommend, if we can't find a way to increase revenues in those areas. I'd explore whether closing our unprofitable large plants and serving their respective customer base is possible with one of our other facilities, preferably a portable facility. My hypothesis is that the large-sized facilities are unprofitable because they are underutilized. If we can't increase business in those plants then we could replace them with portables that run at optimum capacity or via a nearby large-sized facility that has capacity, we could still get the revenues while reducing our costs.

– So what affect do you think this will have on our client's business?

Here are the steps I would take. First, if we shut down the unprofitable large-sized plants, could we serve those customers via other facilities? I'd look at the effect these closings would have on reducing our costs such as rent, insurance, salaries,

utilities, and property taxes. I'd also look at the new costs we'd take on by replacing these facilities – whether with portables or by increasing output of nearby plants.

> – What else would you recommend?

Now that we've looked at the fixed costs, I would like to understand our client's variable costs so I can determine some recommendations on that front also.

> – We are actually running short on time. What avenues would you suggest we explore on the variable cost side?

I would start by digging deeper into which variables costs are out of line versus corresponding benchmarks and which have increased? I'd then look at opportunities to reduce some of those costs – whether through implementation of technology, volume purchasing, hedging, etc.

+ Case 4: Pricing

Our client is a U.S. medical device manufacturer who has invented an innovative artificial valve for an alternative procedure to open-heart surgery called TAVR (Transcatheter Aortic Valve Replacement). TAVR has been proven in clinical trials to be more effective and safer than open-heart surgery. Similarly, for this procedure, our client's valve has been tested and proven to be more successful by the national regulatory bodies than their competitors' respective artificial valves. They have come to us to figure out how much they should price their valve. They would like to achieve a marginal ROI of 4:1 but are not sure if that's feasible.

To summarize, our client wants to know how much they should price their artificial valve used in a new, innovative procedure proven to be safer and more effective than open-heart surgery. Besides achieving a marginal ROI of 4:1 are there any other objectives?

> – No, there are no additional objectives. Just make sure that the price is reasonable.

So we are limited not only by the number of times TAVR is performed over open-heart surgery but also by the number of times our valve is used versus the competition's. I'd like to take a minute to think about my structure.

The student writes out her structure.

I would like to explore a few fronts. First, I'd like to understand the size of the opportunity. That is, how many people are candidates, how fast the market is growing, etc. Second, I'd like to understand our cost structure. Third, what direct or indirect competitive products are there, and how are they priced? Let's start with the market size. Who are the right candidates for this surgery, how many candidates are there in the U.S., and how is that population growing?

– Ideal candidates are those that are high risk for open-heart surgery for their valve replacement. This would be people over the age of 75. Currently, it is estimated that there are 20,000 candidates in the U.S. in need of a new heart valve. With an aging population, that number is expected to grow steadily by about a thousand candidates per year.

I would like to calculate potential revenues. Do we have growth projections for the next decade or so?

– Take a look at this graph.

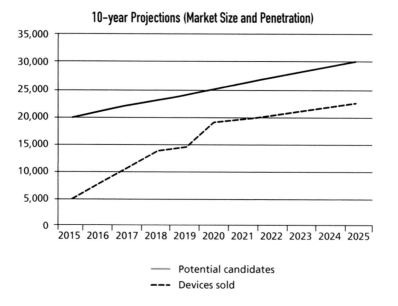

10-year Projections (Market Size and Penetration)

⎯⎯⎯ Potential candidates
--- Devices sold

It looks like we're expecting steady growth in the market, which aligns with the growing population. Also, because the two lines are converging a little after 2017, we are expecting our penetration to increase. Is that because we expect more and more doctors trained and more doctors to prefer TAVR over open-heart surgery so that when they do, they prefer our client's valve to the competition's?

– That's right.

And what can you tell me about our client's costs and investments?

– To date, the client has spent $200M in R&D and another $50M in training 50% of cardiac surgeons in the U.S. in performing TAVR using their device.

Are these doctors loyal to our client's brand? That is, if a patient were to need the TAVR procedure, would these doctors use our client's product?

– Mostly. They should because our client's valve is far superior to competitive products.

Can I assume that our client is willing to spend another $50M to train the rest of the cardiac surgeon population? It seems as if the name of the game is getting doctors on board with your product.

– Yes, our client will try to train the rest of the surgeon population, but keep in mind that the competition is doing the same thing.

So all in, can I assume that our fixed costs are $300M: $200M in R&D and another $100M in marketing/training doctors?

– That's fair.

Now, I would like to focus on our variable costs. Can you give me a breakdown of our variables costs?

– Our variable costs consist primarily of salaries and commissions for our salespeople.

How many salespeople do we currently have, would they sell this valve exclusively, and what is their compensation?

– A salesperson makes $50K base and Finance has approved awarding 10% commissions of the selling price of this valve or revenues. Yes, a salesperson would be dedicated to selling this device only. As you can see, they are placing a big bet on this product. The client believes a salesperson can sell 50 valves a year so it will ramp up the sales force as sales increase

That makes sense. I'd like to shift focus on the competitive marketplace. How many other products are there in the market? I imagine safety and longevity are critical. How does our client's device compare with these in terms of safety, and how much longer do they increase a patient's longevity? Lastly, since the name of the game is getting doctors to install your device, can you tell me how our client's penetration compares with our competitors'?

– Sure. There are two competitors. But studies show our client's device to be safer. Trials also reveal that patients with our device live an additional 12 months. Here is a graph that lays this out.

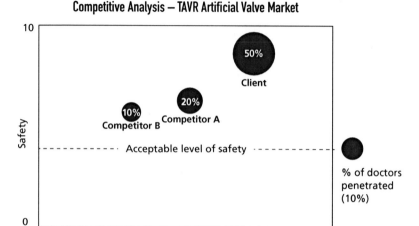

Competitive Analysis – TAVR Artificial Valve Market

Thanks. Do we know how much Competitor A and Competitor B are pricing their device?

– Our client believes B is pricing it at $25K/unit.

Ok. That's very helpful. Given our product's superiority in terms of safety and longevity, I don't think we should price it below $25K. Since the market is already willing to pay that much for it, we know that it can pay at least that much for a better device. Just so I remember correctly, the price needs to allow a minimum ROI of 4:1, right?

– That's correct. Management wants to price it such that the marginal ROI is at least 4:1 over the next 10 years. They want to make sure it's a realistic price.

Ok. For me to figure out the price, I'm going to need some exact numbers against the first chart you gave me.

– Let me speed things up. Assume that we sell 200,000 units over the next 10 years. Evenly distributed over those 10 years.

That helps. With that many units, the total salary paid (in today's dollars) would be calculated as described below, 200,000 units divided by 10 years equals 20,000 units a year. 20,000 units divided by 50 units/salesperson equals 400 sales reps at $50,000 salary is total salary of $20 million. If we sell each unit at $25,000 then we'd have 200,000 times $25,000 and that would equal $5 billion in sales. Which means a 10 percent commission is $500 million. So...

$500M in commission plus $20M in salary plus $350M in fixed costs equals $870 M. The marginal ROI in this case is revenues – costs / costs. (5B – 870M) / 870M equals = 4.13B / .870B = 4.7 well above the 4:1 ROI.

– That's right. Great work. So what's your recommendation?

My recommendation for management would be to price the device at $25K/valve. This allows us to achieve the marginal ROI that management wants. It is also a price that is realistic to charge since a competitor is already charging $25K/device.

✦ Case 5: Pricing

Our client, Apollo Corporation, rents out and launders linen and other textiles to the healthcare industry. Specifically, the company picks up soiled linen from hospitals, takes the soiled linen to its service center for laundry (i.e., processing), and delivers clean linen back to hospitals for their use. Each year, the company directly sources manufacturing of millions of dollars of linen. Bulk purchasing enables Apollo to offer attractive prices – allowing it to compete in a competitive industry. To differentiate it from competitors, Apollo's marketing department is contemplating launching an anti-bacterial bed sheet that will help hospitals in their fight against infections. They would like us to recommend the rent price for this new anti-bacterial bed sheet.

Thank you. To summarize, our client wants us to recommend the rental price for a new anti-bacterial bed sheet that they will rent out to hospitals. Are there any other goals or objectives I should focus on here?

– No you've got it.

I'd like to take a minute to layout my thoughts.

The student takes 40 seconds to layout her thoughts.

I'd like to look at the company, its customers, products, revenues and costs. Then I'd like to look at the industry, particularly our direct competition and whether anyone else offers this product and what they charge.

– Okay, where would you like to start?

Before I focus the analysis on cost, I would like to learn about the products and customers. What products do we have in our portfolio, and would adding this new type of bed sheet entail purchasing new equipment?

– Apollo has a wide range of products in its portfolio, including bed sheets, thermal blankets, pillowcases, hand towels, washcloths, bath towels, patient gowns, scrubs, and lab coats. Each item is processed or laundered in a state-of-the-art facility fitted with the latest industrial washing equipment. The new bed sheet can be processed using existing equipment and current detergents and thus will not require installation of additional capacity. It is believed that the new sheet will cannibalize sales of the existing flat sheet.

Ok. That's good to know. What can you tell me about our client's customer base? Will having this allow us to target a new segment?

– The base wouldn't change at all. We would be renting these out to the same customer, namely large hospitals.

What's the company's pricing objective? Is it a certain margin or increased market share?

– I'd say it is to increase revenues. Again this is a very competitive market and we want to make sure that we retain our current customers and maybe pick up a few new ones.

There are several pricing strategies. Cost-based, value-based, and competitive-based are three that come to mind. This seems to be a commoditized industry. If so, it seems as if cost-based pricing is the best approach. Am I on the right track?

– Yes, your hunch is correct. In fact, our client is in a highly commoditized industry so cost-based pricing is the best approach here. One thing to keep in mind is that our client bills on a weekly basis and only for the quantities delivered.

Thanks. I'd like to focus on our costs. What are our variable costs?

– Why don't you figure it out? Let me describe the activities to help you. Our client purchases product from different suppliers. Then it processes it. Finally, once it's clean and folded, our client delivers the product to its customers.

That's helpful. So, I'm guessing our variable costs are merchandise, processing, and delivery costs. Let me start with merchandise costs. You mentioned that this is a rental business where our client bills on what it delivers. So, I'm assuming we should arrive at a cost on a "per use" basis. Can you tell me what our merchandise cost is for this new bed sheet?

– You're absolutely right. This is a rental business so each cost should be on a "per use" basis. Each use is referred to in the industry as a "turn." So, if Apollo's unit cost for an item is $20, and the item gets 20 turns, its merchandise cost is $1. Apollo will source this product from four suppliers. Each supplier's product has a different cost, and in wash-testing, each is proven to have different durability. In other words, each bed sheet has a set number of turns before it wears out and must be replaced.

Can you tell me the average number of turns? Also, how many units are purchased from each supplier?

– Take a look at this graph. Our client buys 100K units from A, 150K from B, 250K from C, and 250K from D.

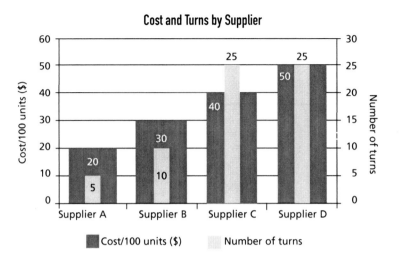

Cost and Turns by Supplier

The student takes a minute to layout and fill in this chart.

Based on this data, our total cost is $290K and the total number of turns we could get is 14.5M. Therefore, our merchandise cost per turn is $0.02.

	Units Bought	Cost/100 Units	Total Cost	Turns/Unit	Total Turns
Supplier A	100,000	$20.00	$20,000.00	5	500,000
Supplier B	150,000	$30.00	$45,000.00	10	1,500,000
Supplier C	250,000	$40.00	$100,000.00	25	6,250,000
Supplier D	250,000	$50.00	$125,000.00	25	6,250,000
Total			$290,000.00		14,500,000
					$0.0200

– That's good.

Now let's move on to processing cost. What can you tell me about our processing costs?

– Before we go there, what do you think processing involves?

I suppose processing involves everything that takes place from the time the soiled linen comes into our facility to the time it leaves the facility. I would guess the individual steps are sorting, washing, drying, and folding.

– That is exactly correct. I can't tell you each individual step's cost, but you can figure that out.

Ok. I suspect all four involve energy and human labor. Is that correct?

– Take a look at these waterfalls. These should make things clear.

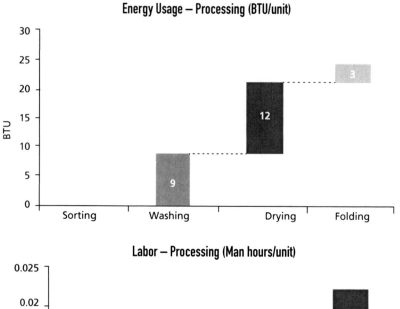

Energy Usage – Processing (BTU/unit)

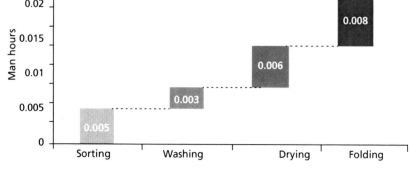

Labor – Processing (Man hours/unit)

It seems as if sorting involves only labor. The remaining three carry an energy and manual component to them. What wage do we pay hourly, and what are our energy costs?

– We pay $10/man hour and our energy costs are $0.01/BTU.

The student takes a minute to layout and fill in this chart.

Using these graphs, I get to $0.46/unit for processing costs. Here is my work:

	Electricity usage (BTU)	Electricity cost	Labor hours	Labor costs
Sorting	0	$0.00	0.005	$0.05
Washing	9	$0.09	0.003	$0.03
Drying	12	$0.12	0.006	$0.06
Folding	3	$0.03	0.008	$0.08
Total		$0.24		$0.22
				$0.46

– That's absolutely correct. What's next?

Let's finish up with delivery costs. What are the different costs comprising delivery cost? In other words, what are the drivers having a material impact on the delivery cost?

– What do you think are the different components?

Are our drivers salaried, and how do we deliver our linen?

– Our drivers are salaried at $8/hour. They work 8 hours/day. We deliver our linen on a truck that we lease. The monthly lease amount is $400/truck.

Ok, so our fixed costs are salary and truck lease. Any other fixed costs?

– No.

What about our variable costs? How many miles does an average truck travel/day roundtrip? What's the fuel efficiency of a truck? How much is gas, and how many routes does a truck make per day? Finally, how many units are delivered per day per route?

– All good questions. The daily route on average is 50 miles roundtrip. On average, our trucks get 10 miles/gallon. Gas is $2/gallon, and on average our truck takes makes 10 routes/day. Also, we would deliver 50 bed sheets per route per day.

Thank you.

The student takes a minute to layout and fill in this chart.

So here is what I would do to figure out the delivery cost/unit.

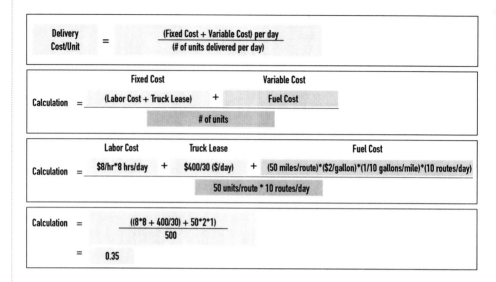

So my total unit cost = Merchandise cost + Processing cost + Delivery cost or $0.02 + $0.46 + $0.35 or $0.83. Now that I know the unit cost, I'd like to know if we have any competitive pricing.

– Unfortunately, we don't because we are currently the only provider in our industry.

I see. Do we have any clinical data showing the value of this sheet? That is, will having the sheet reduce infections, each of which has a cost associated with it, and how much is that cost?

– Unfortunately, we don't have that information either.

Ok. What is the price of our regular, non anti-bacterial bed sheet?

– The regular sheet – priced 20% lower than this sheet's fully-loaded cost – provides a 30% gross margin.

Well, if we want similar margins, we should use gross up the $0.83. If we do that, we get 1.3 x $0.83 or $1.08.

– So what is your recommendation?

Since we are the only company offering this type of sheet, and presumably, it's desired in the market, we should be able to command this margin – at least until there is competition.

+ Case 6: Feasibility — Apollo Corporation Revisited

Previously, we were working with Apollo Corporation who came to us with a recommendation on pricing their innovative anti-bacterial bed sheet. Through our analysis, we came up with a price that Apollo had little trouble selling to their hospital clients. As a result of that successful engagement, we were able to secure follow-on work. This new engagement, Apollo's CEO is interested in finding out the next steps in assessing the size of the opportunity in the US. How would you suggest that the CEO team should go about it?

It's great that we got follow-on work. To be clear, the CEO wants us to size the opportunity. Are there any other objectives?

— One additional objective. After sizing the opportunity, the CEO wants to know our recommendation on moving forward.

Ok. That's helpful to know. Give me a second to write down my thoughts.

The student takes 30 seconds.

To gauge the opportunity, I'd structure the analysis by looking at what competing products there are in the market, the benefits that differentiate our product, our ability to finance this investment, the impact on cannibalization, the size of the customer base, and our capacity limitations.

— Those are all the key factors, and you are correct in looking into those components. Let me provide some additional information to help guide your thinking. On the product side, we are the only anti-bacterial sheet provider in this space. In other words, our competitors aren't offering it yet, but there is no reason to believe that they cannot since we don't have exclusivity deals in place with our suppliers. The benefits of our sheet are fairly evident. They have a coating that kills bacteria that can infect patients as they lay on the bed. With respect to our client's ability to finance this, they are presently cash-rich so financing this isn't an issue for them. Currently, we're planning on using these sheets on beds in specific, high-risk wings of the hospital where they currently use paper. As such, introducing this bed sheet into our product portfolio poses no cannibalization threat. I would encourage you to focus on the customer base and our capacity.

Thank you for the context. I'd like to focus on customer demand. What can you tell me about our customer base? How many hospitals are there in the U.S. with beds that are eligible for this innovative bed sheet?

– Take a look at this graph.

% of Eligible Hospital Beds by Region

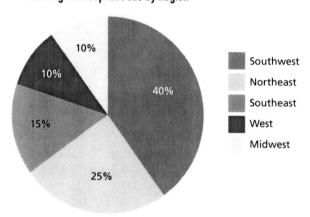

This is a geographic distribution of the number of beds within our client's customer base. How many total hospital beds does our client serve in the U.S., and how many of these sheets would be needed per week, per bed?

– There are 500,000 hospital beds in the U.S. In terms of sheets per bed, our client has collected some sample data of its own facilities that may help you.

Distribution of Sheets Used Per Bed

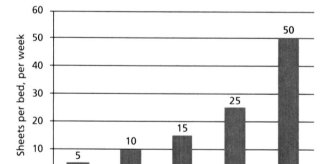

So if I'm interpreting this correctly, we sampled 10% of our base and this subset shows the number of sheets used per week by a particular number of beds. For example, there were 10,000 beds that used 5 sheets in a week.

– That's correct.

Ok, so based on my math, the average number of sheets per week per bed is 20.

Beds	Sheets/bed-week	Sheets
10,000	5	50,000
10,000	15	150,000
20,000	25	500,000
5,000	50	250,000
5,000	10	50,000
50,000		1,000,000
Avg number of sheets/week-bed		20.0

– Right again.

Using 500,000 hospital beds in the country, our geographic distribution of beds, and 20 sheets per week per bed, I arrive at 10M sheets. In the previous case, we calculated an average price per sheet at $1.08, but if we round that to $1.10, that equates to a weekly $11M opportunity.

Region	Share of beds	Beds served by Apollo	Sheets/week
SW	40%	200,000	4,000,000
NE	25%	125,000	2,500,000
SE	15%	75,000	1,500,000
W	10%	50,000	1,000,000
MW	10%	50,000	1,000,000
Total		500,000	10,000,000
Price/sheet			$1.10
Opportunity			11,000,000

– Pretty good. What do you want to do now?

I'd like to determine if we can actually serve this demand to realize the full value of the opportunity. What can you tell me about our current capacity?

– We currently have 50 plants throughout the country. Each facility has excess capacity to process an additional 100,000 sheets/week.

How are these plants distributed geographically?

– Here you go.

% of Apollo's Facilities by Geographic Region

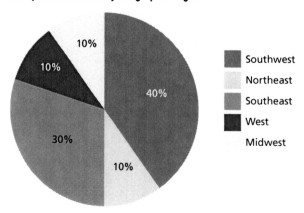

- Southwest
- Northeast
- Southeast
- West
- Midwest

Doing the math, I see that we can only capture about half of the opportunity or $5.5M/week, which is not bad.

Region	# of plants	Sheets/week
SW	20	2,000,000
NE	5	500,000
SE	15	1,500,000
W	5	500,000
MW	5	500,000
Total	50	5,000,000
Price/sheet		$1.10
Opportunity		$5,500,000

What I would like to determine is how much we can capture in each region, and where we may want to consider investing.

According to my math, the only region where we can fulfill demand is the Southeast.

Region	Share of beds	Beds served by Apollo	Sheets/week	# of plants	Sheets/week	Variance
SW	40%	200,000	4,000,000	20	2,000,000	(2,000,000)
NE	25%	125,000	2,500,000	5	500,000	(2,000,000)
SE	15%	75,000	1,500,000	15	1,500,000	0
W	10%	50,000	1,000,000	5	500,000	(500,000)
MW	10%	50,000	1,000,000	5	500,000	(500,000)
Total		500,000	10,000,000	50	5,000,000	(5,000,000)
Price/sheet			$1.10		$1.10	
Opportunity			$11,000,000		$5,500,000	(5,500,000)

    – So what is your recommendation?

I would state that while the market opportunity is $11M weekly, our excess capacity only enables us to capture half of it. We could invest in building a plant that allows us to capture the rest of this, but that level of investment should also consider market demand beyond anti-bacterial bed sheets.

✛ Case 7: Market Entry

Our client is one of the top hotel companies in the world. Traditionally, they have catered to the business market with an upper-tier offering for business travelers that has garnered them much respect among this consumer segment. In addition to their offering in the upper-tier category, the company has brands in most of the other categories to appeal to a wider consumer base. A new category called the "Boutique" segment has recently emerged, and our client has asked us to recommend whether or not they should enter this category.

I'd like to reiterate the facts of the case as well as my understanding of our objectives. Our client is a large hotel company with offerings in all hotel categories except for the newly-created Boutique segment. They want our recommendation on whether or not they should enter this category. With this offering, is their primary objective to grow revenue?

    – Yup. That's right. I wouldn't worry about costs. They are sitting on a lot of cash at the moment since they are the dominant player among business travelers who want to stay in an upper-tier hotel.

Ok. I'd like to base my recommendation by first understanding the Boutique category. I would then focus on the competitive landscape. I'd then evaluate customer demand and consumer demand. Finally, I'd size the revenue potential of the market to round out my recommendation.

– That sounds like a solid plan.

You alluded to different categories in the hotel space. Can you explain what you mean? This will help me understand where and how the boutique segment fits.

– Sure, the graph below shows the different categories.

CHART

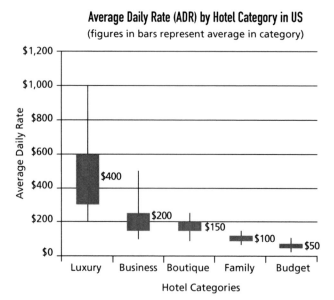

Average Daily Rate (ADR) by Hotel Category in US
(figures in bars represent average in category)

Average Daily Rate

- $400
- $200
- $150
- $100
- $50

Luxury   Business   Boutique   Family   Budget

Hotel Categories

This is very helpful. Based on the chart above, it appears as if the Boutique category bridges the Average Daily Rate gap between the Business category, where the average daily rate is $200 and the Family category, where the average daily rate is $100. For hotel companies with an offering in this category, this could help them capture buyer's surplus of a consumer willing to pay more than $100 but not quite as much as $200. What can you tell me about the consumer's experience in a Boutique hotel?

– Boutique hotels have a very unique décor or style to them. They do not resemble "big box" chains that are very "cookie-cutter." Boutiques are catered to business travelers who want a little more personality in their hotels. These hotels are not full-service hotels like Business hotels, but they are very comfortable and luxurious in their own right.

I can see why our client would be interested in having an offering, but I would like to understand if it makes sense from a competitive perspective. Can you tell me currently how many competitors there are in the Boutique space and what their share is in terms of annual revenues and total number of rooms?

– Here is a graph that provides that information.

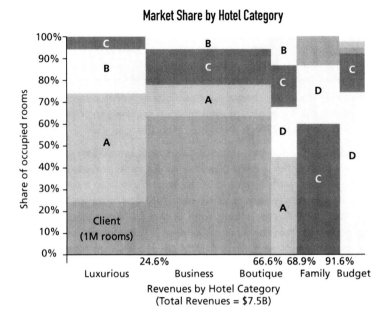

Market Share by Hotel Category

(Share of occupied rooms vs. Revenues by Hotel Category, Total Revenues = $7.5B)

Categories along the horizontal axis: Luxurious, Business (24.6%), Boutique (66.6%), Family (68.9%), Budget (91.6%)

Client (1M rooms)

– And here is the underlying data.

| | ADR | Occupied Room | | | |
		Client	A	B	C	D
Luxurious	$400	1,000,000	2,000,000	1,000,000	100,000	
Business	$200	10,000,000	2,000,000	1,000,000	2,000,000	
Boutique	$150		500,000	100,000	200,000	250,000
Family	$100	2,000,000			10,000,000	5,000,000
Budget	$55	200,000	2,000,000	100,000	1,000,000	10,000,000

Business hotels clearly provide the bulk of the revenues of the entire industry with our client leading the way with 10 million occupied rooms annually. Even though all four of our competitors have entered the Boutique space, the category as a whole only accounts for $157.5M in annual revenues (1,050,000 occupied rooms x $150 average daily rate). Thus, none of the competitors are placing a "big bet" in the Boutique category yet so the competitive intensity should not scare us. Moreover, just because the competition has a head start does not mean that their strategy is sound.

I'd like to shift my focus on customer and consumer demand. Since the hotel industry is one where each property is privately owned and the owner provides a royalty and management fee to the brand, I assume our customers are owner and our consumers are hotel guests. Is that correct?

– That's right.

So, what can you tell me about interest from the owner community as regards boutique hotels?

– Our client actually met with each and every current owner to gauge their interest level. With the exception of some owners who own properties in the Family category, most owners loved the idea of a boutique hotel. Several indicated wanting to purchase our client's boutique offering once it became available. Our client also ran focus groups with business travelers to collect their thoughts about boutique hotels. Most, if not all, loved the idea.

There is very compelling evidence to pursue this space, but I'd like to run some numbers to ensure that this is still a good opportunity for us to pursue. I am going to make some assumptions. Let's assume that the total number of rooms is constant if we entered the Boutique category. In other words, just because we have a Boutique offering, we're not going to create new hotel guests. Let's also assume that we'll cannibalize some rooms from the Business category. These would be more price-sensitive consumers who would rather pay $150/night for fewer services than the $200 they are currently paying. I'll also assume that some guests from the Family category are going to "upgrade" to the Boutique category. These are guests who prefer a better hotel than a Family hotel but do not want to pay $200. Are these valid assumptions?

– Yes, I like how you're thinking about this. What's next?

To calculate the change in revenues, I need to estimate how much our Boutique offering is going to impact our occupied rooms in the Business and Family categories. Can you provide this information?

– We looked at how it impacted our competitors and here is what we learned.

	Competitor A		Competitor B		Competitor C		Competitor D	
	Before	After	Before	After	Before	After	Before	After
Business rooms	2,500,000	2,000,000	1,100,000	1,000,000	2,100,000	2,000,000	0	0
Family rooms		0		0	10,100,000	10,000,000	5,250,000	5,000,000

I'd like to spend a minute calculating the average decline in the number of occupied rooms for both categories.

– Sure.

Based on my math, decline in the number of occupied rooms in the Business category was 12.3%, and the decline in the Family category was 2.3%. Are those correct?

– Yes. Your math is dead on.

Thanks. I would like to take a stab at how our revenues would be impacted if we entered the Boutique space. This would be once we reached steady state because we wouldn't enter all at once. Based on the first graph you showed me, our annual occupied rooms and revenues per category are:

Category	Average Daily Rate	Rooms	Revenues
Luxurious	$400	1,000,000	$400,000,000
Business	$200	10,000,000	$2,000,000,000
Boutique	$150	0	$0
Family	$100	2,000,000	$200,000,000
Budget	$55	200,000	$10,000,000
Total		13,200,000	$2,610,000,000

Assuming a 12.3% decline in the number of occupied rooms in our Business hotels and a 2.3% decline in the number of occupied rooms in our Family hotels, I'm seeing that our annual revenues actually take a slide dip.

- To make the math easier, assume 10% instead of 12.3% and 2% instead of 2.3%.

Category	Average Daily Rate	Rooms	Revenues
Luxurious	$400	1,000,000	$400,000,000
Business	$200	9,000,000	$1,800,000,000
Boutique	$150	1,040,000	$156,000,000
Family	$100	1,960,000	$196,000,000
Budget	$55	200,000	$10,000,000
Total		13,200,000	$2,562,000,000

- Interesting. So what is your recommendation?

Based on pure revenues, it would appear as if this is not a wise move. However, we don't know how our profits would be impacted. Our Family hotels may be unprofitable so taking some unprofitable capacity out of the portfolio might be a good thing. Also, Boutique hotels – because they aren't full-service – may have a lower cost structure, making them more profitable. We also do not know whether or not there is demand for another ~1M occupied rooms – both from owners and from consumers. My recommendation, strictly on the basis of revenues, would be to postpone entering the market. If, however, we did an analysis looking at profitability, this may be a good investment.

+ Case 8: Business Expansion

Our client is one of the top healthcare insurers in the United States in terms of members. Given the changes taking place in healthcare, namely the Affordable Care Act, the uninsured population presents a significant opportunity to our client to expand its business and achieve growth. Historically, they have catered to the employer market, but given the changes coming out of Washington, they have hired us to determine the size of the opportunity among individual insurance buyers and recommend whether we should pursue this segment.

Thank you for the background. So, just to confirm the objectives, our client is a large insurance company whose main clientele consisted of employers. They are looking to expand into the individual market because of political changes. They have hired us to determine the size of the opportunity and whether we should pursue it. So, is their goal to achieve top-line growth?

– Yes. That's right. Under the Affordable Care Act, Americans who are uninsured are required to purchase private insurance or face a penalty.

Are there any other objectives I should be concerned with?

– No.

Ok. I would like to take a moment to structure my thoughts.

The student takes 60 seconds to layout her structure.

I'd like to frame my recommendation by first understanding the uninsured consumer. Next, I want to focus on the economics of pursuing this segment and our potential return. Finally, I would like to explore what organizational capabilities we have to move forward. My hypothesis is that expanding into this new marketplace would be profitable.

– Sounds good. Where do you want to start?

What can you tell me about the uninsured consumer? Let's start with how many Americans are uninsured.

– Here is a graph of the uninsured population based on research by our client's analytics department.

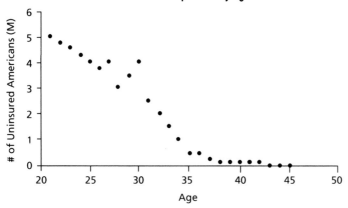

US Uninsured Population by Age

So based on this, there seems to be a strong linear negative relationship between age and the uninsured population. There are a couple of outliers around the age of 30, but for the most part, as people age, they seem to have insurance – whether through their employers or independently. Am I correct to assume that there are approximately 50M uninsured Americans and that the majority of them are under the age of 30?

– That's correct. Good observation. There are about 40M adults under the age of 30 that do not have any health insurance. How would you like to proceed now?

I'd like to dig deeper into the under-30 uninsured population. Do we have any data on this age group to understand what drives their purchase decision and what their propensity is to purchase insurance in the face of federal regulation?

– Our client's marketing department has conducted market research on this population and it seems that marital status and an individual's own perception of his or her general health impact the insurance purchase decision. Here is the output of that research.

% of Segment Likely to Purchase Insurance

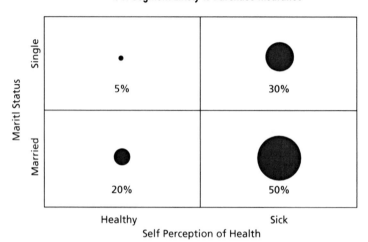

This is very helpful. As one would expect, one's perception of one's health is a huge factor in purchasing healthcare. Those who are married are more likely, which makes sense also. Since this is the percentage of each segment that is likely to purchase insurance, I'd like to know the population of each of these segments so I can proceed with evaluating the economics of this potential effort.

- Sure, here you go.

Population Breakout (<30 years of age)

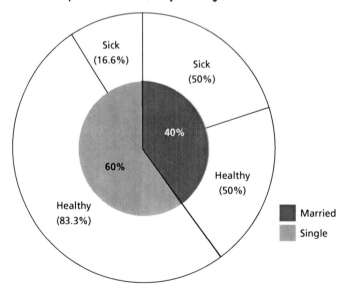

As I size the opportunity, I would like to know our market share, the value of a new customer in terms of revenues, and the cost or payout per customer.

- Good questions. "Lifetime" is considered to be one year since people can switch every year. On average, we believe the lifetime value is $10K for single individuals and $15K for married couples. Our market share is 20%. In terms of costs or payout per customer, here is a breakdown.

	Per Customer	
Segment	Revenues	Cost or Payout
Single-sick	$10,000	$5,000
Single-healthy	$10,000	$2,000
Married-sick	$10,000	$8,000
Married-healthy	$10,000	$5,000

So I think I have what I need to calculate the revenues we can expect. I'm going to need a moment to figure this out.

The student refers to all the given graphs and then takes two minutes to make this chart.

Here is my work. Based on this analysis, it seems as if this is a worthwhile investment.

Segment	Mkt size	Pop. (M)	Purchase intent %	Potential customers (M)	Our Share (20%)	Value/ cust.	Revenues ($B)	Cost or Payout/ cust.	Total Costs (B)
Single-sick	10%	4 M	30%	1.2 M	.24M	$10,000	$2.4B	$5,000	$1.2B
Single-healthy	50%	20M	5%	1 M	.2M	$10,000	$2B	$2,000	$.4B
Married-sick	20%	8M	50%	4 M	.8M	$15,000	$12B	$8,000	$6.4B
Married-healthy	20%	8M	20%	1.6M	.32M	$15,000	$4.8B	$5,000	$1.6B
Total							$21.2B		$9.6B

- This is pretty good, but if our share is 20%, shouldn't we naturally achieve these results without any effort. Is this the true representation of our results?

You bring up an excellent point. We should, in fact, get these with our share where it is in the market. What we should really care about is the lift due to our efforts. To figure that out, I'm going to need to know the lift we've been able to achieve historically due to our marketing efforts.

- Our client's previous investments in marketing have seen an incremental lift of about 5%.

Ok. So, would a safe assumption be to estimate 3% lift across all four segments? For example, can I estimate the incremental – in the case of the single-sick population – to be 3% of 1.2M or 36K?

- That's right.

The student writes out a new chart.

Ok, in that case, the incremental revenues and costs would be:

Segment	Potential Customers	Incremental Customers	Incremental Revenues	Incremental Costs
Single-sick	1,200,000	36,000	$360,000,000	$180,000,000
Single-healthy	1,000,000	30,000	$300,000,000	$60,000,000
Married-sick	4,000,000	120,000	$1,800,000,000	$960,000,000
Married-healthy	1,600,000	48,000	$720,000,000	$240,000,000
Total			$3,180,000,000	$1,440,000,000

- This is perfect. What's next?

So, what can you tell me about our client's ability to target married individuals under the age of 30? I'd like to hyper-target those since the margins on this sub-segment is the greatest – as are the incremental revenues.

- Let's assume that our client has the business intelligence infrastructure and the organizational structure to execute this successfully. What's your recommendation?

My first recommendation would you to prioritize the under 30 married segment. I'd then try to figure out how I can hyper-target this segment through cost-effective tactics and channels. Because I would want to lower my costs, I recommend coming up with wellness programs that would prevent these individuals from getting sick in the first place.

About the Authors

Marc Cosentino

Cosentino is the CEO of CaseQuestions.com. Over the past 25 years he has advised and coached over 100,000 students and alumni. He has written four books involving cases and consulting. *Case in Point* is now published in four languages and was called the "MBA Bible" by the *Wall Street Journal*. Cosentino has traveled nationwide giving workshops to students at colleges and graduate programs and has held training sessions for career services professionals. He has consulted with and designed cases for private sector firms, government agencies and non-profits.

Cosentino is a graduate of Harvard's Kennedy School, Harvard's Program on Negotiation and the University of Denver.

Mukund Jain

Having spent several years as a management consultant including a stint at The Boston Consulting Group, Mukund developed a strong interest in data interpretation and its visual representation. After consulting, Mukund worked in industry in various strategy roles where he strengthened his analytical skills and refined the data interpretation framework discussed in this book. A graduate of Duke University, the University of Michigan, and Harvard University, Mukund enjoys spending time with his wife Garima and son Shaunak in Atlanta.

CPSIA information can be obtained at www.ICGtesting.com
Printed in the USA
BVOW01s1147170816

459317BV00009B/31/P